MILESTONES OF THOUGHT

Literature and Dogma
MATTHEW ARNOLD

Edited, abridged, and with an introduction by

JAMES C. LIVINGSTON
The College of William and Mary

Frederick Ungar Publishing Co.
New York

MILESTONES
OF THOUGHT
in the History of Ideas

Editor's Introduction

The 1860s and '70s in England remain one of the most interesting periods in the long conflict between Christianity and the movements of modern secular thought. Outwardly it appeared to be an age of conspicuous religious faith, but beneath the surface mid-Victorian England was seething with religious uncertainty and conflict. Christianity was losing its hold on many of the finest minds of the day—men and women who had been raised in the bosom of Evangelicalism or who, as students, had been drawn to Anglo-Catholicism at Oxford by scholars like John Henry Newman and E. B. Pusey. Some of these sensitive spirits were abandoning the Christian faith because of what they came to consider the crude and inhumane teachings of the church on such matters as the sacrificial atonement and eternal damnation. But most of those in the educated class who turned from Christianity did so because of the gulf created between them and their religious creed by what Matthew Arnold called the *Zeitgeist;* i.e., the scientific advance and its demand for a new warrant for traditional belief. With the progress of the natural and historical sciences more and more of the accepted grounds of Christian belief were being challenged and rejected.

The conflict between deeply-ingrained religious feelings and a scrupulous devotion to the search for truth produced in many of the leading Victorian figures a tension, even fracture, which makes fascinating the study of their life and thought. Many of these men of letters never entirely shed certain fundamental Christian assumptions while denying most of the traditional Christian beliefs. The old dogmas no longer satisfied, and yet for these men there was a yearning and a sense of loss. They waited expectantly for some new meaning to emerge. For them it was, indeed, a time

> between two worlds, one dead
> The other powerless to be born.

Other more militant freethinkers, like Frederick Harrison, W. K. Clifford, and Leslie Stephen, believed they had discovered the new and truer grounds for hope in an unbiased devotion to the method and evidences of Science.

Matthew Arnold was among a small band who, while convinced that the doctrines were grossly inadequate, if not entirely untenable, nevertheless believed that Christianity remained mankind's truest and most satisfying religious creed. In 1875 Arnold expressed this conviction in the Preface to *God and the Bible* where he wrote:

> At the present moment two things about the Christian religion must surely be clear to anybody with eyes in his head. One is, that men cannot do without it; the other, that they cannot do with it as it is.

Arnold's dual commitment to the Christian religion and to the higher culture places him in the long and estimable tradition of Christian humanism. Like the humanist Erasmus in the sixteenth century, and others before and since, Arnold combined a seemingly paradoxical devotion to the Christian tradition and to what appeared to many to be radically advanced ideas. He was both committed to the eternal verities he found enshrined in the Bible and unstinting in his loyalty to critical freedom in the study of the biblical literature. Arnold was, in the words of Basil Willey, "a conservative-reforming force," and as such representative of the best of nineteenth-century thought.

As in the case of Erasmus, Arnold's balance of conservative and advanced tendencies was frequently interpreted by both the orthodox and the freethinkers as a temporizing weakness. In fact, this dual commitment of Arnold's reflected his awareness of the necessity of achieving a reconciliation between Christianity and modern learning; that is, if the age was to escape both the deadening influence of the new positivism and materialism, as well as the intolerance and obscurantism of those religionists who possessed zeal without knowledge. In the 1870s Matthew Arnold found himself thrust in the role of spokesman for a position that would find little favor with the traditional defenders of the faith or their rationalist and positivist critics.

II

A series of events, beginning with the Colenso affair of 1862, played a decisive role in Arnold's decision to devote his energies to the religious controversies of his time by writing a series of articles for the *Cornhill* magazine. Some understanding of these issues and Arnold's response to them should enhance the reader's understanding of *Literature and Dogma*.

In 1862 Dr. J. W. Colenso, Bishop of Natal, published the first volume of a work entitled *The Pentateuch and Book of Joshua Critically Examined*. Colenso had served as a Fellow and Tutor at Cambridge and was the author of several texts on mathematics. After leaving Cambridge he was sent by the Church of England to a remote bishopric in South Africa. There he began a translation of parts of the Old Testament into Zulu. A question put to him by a native assistant concerning the factual reliability of the story of Noah and the Flood revived Colenso's earlier doubts about the historicity of portions of the Old Testament, doubts that he had for the time put to rest because of clerical activity.

Colenso had read Charles Lyell's *Elements of Geology* (1838), which had convinced him that a world deluge such as was described by the Hebrew writer of Genesis 6–9 could not have occurred. Newly perplexed, Colenso turned for guidance to the works of the learned German biblical critics. They confirmed his belief that the Pentateuch contained numerous legends and stories filled with impossible and unreliable information, which was being taught as historical fact. The result of this study was Colenso's book on *The Pentateuch*, demonstrating—largely by arithmetical computations—the absurdity of many of the Mosaic narratives. Like a great deal of the rationalist biblical criticism of the mid-nineteenth century, Colenso's book was largely negative. Its minute dissection of each narrative sapped the life blood from the vibrant biblical stories.

Arnold read Colenso's book shortly after its appearance and determined to answer the bishop's "jejune and technical" treatment of the biblical literature. His reply, entitled "The Bishop and the Philosopher," was published in *Macmillan's Magazine* early in 1863 and was immediately opposed by liberals and orthodox alike. In his critique of Colenso, Arnold enunciates a principle of religious criticism that he was to develop a decade later in *Literature and Dogma*; i.e., either a book of religious criticism should edify the masses or it should instruct the intellectual few. In Arnold's view, Colenso's *The Pentateuch* failed to edify, for the bishop's method was simply negative, pouncing on every opportunity to make plain the difficulties of the biblical narrative. Nor did Colenso further instruct the educated with his elaborate mathematical demonstrations. They were already well aware of the incongruities and legends that abound in the early books of the Bible; that many of these stories were not to be taken as factual, historical events. But the essential issue was entirely missed, for, according to Arnold, the real question is

What then? What follows from all this? What change is it, if true, to produce in the relations of mankind to the Christian religion? If the old theory of Scriptural Inspiration is to be abandoned, what place is the Bible henceforth to hold among books? What is the new Christianity to be like? [1]

[1] "The Bishop and the Philosopher," *Macmillan's Magazine*, VII (Jan., 1863), 246.

These are questions on which the Bishop of Natal never touched. What was lacking in Colenso's work was a sense of what is really important, a sense of *proportion*, which Arnold identified as a necessary quality in the educated man, the *sine qua non* of genuine culture.

For Arnold the true religious critic is one who,

> shutting his mind against no ideas brought by the spirit of his time, sets these ideas, in the sphere of the religious life, in their right prominence, and still puts that first which is first; who under pressure of new thoughts, keeps the center of religious life where it should be.[2]

The failure of Colenso to grasp the real function of the religious critic and Arnold's increasing awareness that Colenso merely represented a growing body of clergymen, liberal and orthodox, was instrumental in his decision to engage himself more directly in the religious disputes of his day.

William Blackburn[3] has shown that there were three religious controversies of the early 1870s that played an especially important role in both Arnold's motivation in writing *Literature and Dogma* and in the content of the book itself.

The first of these issues was the debate over the Forster Education Bill of 1870. The question raised by the bill was whether religious instruction in tax-supported schools should be secular or sectarian—whether, in Arnold's terms, it should be literary or dogmatic. The National Education League was dedicated to a universal public education that would be compulsory and *secular*. Other parties were call-

---

[2] "Dr. Stanley's Lectures on the Jewish Church," *Macmillan's Magazine,* VII (1863), 334.
[3] "The Background of Arnold's Literature and Dogma," *Modern Philology* (Nov., 1945), pp. 130–39. I, as well as many other students of Arnold, am especially indebted to Blackburn for his researches on the immediate background of *Literature and Dogma.*

ing for the inclusion of the catechism and religious formularies in the instruction of the tax-supported schools—a demand that was defeated.

The Forster Education Bill debate was finally to focus on the question of whether and how the Bible should be used as a regular part of the school curriculum. That the issue was no longer a mere "family quarrel" among Christians was remarked by T. H. Huxley, the noted scientist and defender of Darwin, in a speech before the London School Board in February, 1871. Huxley warned the Board that it was a cardinal error to consider the matter of religious instruction as simply an intra-Christian contest. In addition to the Christian antagonists,

there was a third party growing up and daily increasing in significance, which has nothing to do with either, but which has its own religion and morality that rests in no way whatever on the foundation of the other two.[4]

What especially struck Arnold about Huxley's reported speech was the suggestion that this "third party" had lost all allegiance to the Bible. Huxley had remarked that "if these islands had no religion at all, it would not enter into his mind to introduce the religious idea by the agency of the Bible." Arnold was as aware as Huxley of the growing numbers of people for whom the Bible was a mere anachronism, if not a downright evil. But Arnold interpreted this widespread contempt for the Bible as due not only to the new science but to the crude and tortured interpretations of the biblical literature advanced by large numbers of clergymen—men of narrow training, lacking any appreciation of letters.

At the time of the Forster Education Bill debate another controversy was raging that also engaged Arnold's at-

[4] Blackburn, *op. cit.*, p. 133.

tention and influenced substantially the argument of *Literature and Dogma*—especially the book's polemic against "dogmatic" Christianity. Arnold's friend Arthur P. Stanley, the Anglican Dean of Westminster, had invited a Unitarian, named Vance Smith, to receive Holy Communion at Westminster Abbey on June 22, 1870. The occasion was a meeting of a group named by the Convocation of Bishops to consider the question of revising the English version of the Bible. The group included not only Anglicans but Scottish Presbyterians, Nonconformists, and the Unitarian Smith; these men were asked to cooperate in the project because of their eminent scholarship. At the first meeting of the revision committee, Stanley invited all present to participate in the celebration of Holy Communion. High Churchmen were horrified at Stanley's action, which they considered contrary to the rubrics of the Prayer Book that held the vows of confirmation as a prerequisite for receiving Holy Communion. The scandal was brought before Convocation at its next meeting, and letters and memorials poured in denouncing Stanley and demanding his excommunication for such "a gross profanation of the Sacrament."

The controversy reached its zenith at the meeting of Convocation in February, 1871. Bishop Samuel Wilberforce, then of Winchester, moved "that no person who denies the Godhead of our Lord Jesus Christ ought to be invited to join either Company to which is committed the revision of the Authorized Version of Holy Scripture." Wilberforce pointed out that his reason for wishing to exclude Vance Smith was not because he was a separatist from the Church of England, but because he was "a denier of our Lord's Godhead." Wilberforce explained to his peers that in approving his motion,

you enhance in the sight of all your own estimate of the difference between being unhappily separated from your outward community, *but being separated from you in that infinite separation for time and for eternity which is involved in declaring the Eternal*

*Son to be a mere creature; and you have the evidence before you
that he rejects the Godhead of the Eternal Son* [italics added].[5]

Wilberforce's efforts were zealously supported by the
Bishop of Gloucester, who lectured Convocation on the necessity of holding proper conceptions of the personality of
the Holy Trinity, and who shortly thereafter was to write an
essay for a book entitled *Modern Scepticism,* in which he
offered his belief in "the blessed truth that the God of the
universe is a PERSON." It was the action of the Bishops of
Winchester and Gloucester, "in doing something for the
honour of Our Lord's Godhead" (as Arnold was to put it),
and their pretentious claims to know the exact nature of the
Deity that incensed Arnold and brought his mocking wrath
down upon their heads time and time again in *Literature
and Dogma.*

The High Church party's opposition to Stanley did not
end with the meeting of Convocation early in 1871.
Throughout the 1850s and '60s the High Church party had
held the majority of votes in Congregation at Oxford. As a
result, they had long controlled many academic appoint-
ments at the University. During this period distinguished
scholars such as Mark Pattison, Max Müller, and Benjamin
Jowett were denied positions because of their theological
views. The abolition of the Universities Test Act in 1871
reduced the Anglo-Catholic control of Oxford, but their opposition to latitudinarian theology in the University continued unabated. In December, 1872, Dean Stanley was
nominated one of the Select Preachers of the University.
The High Churchmen once again joined forces and were set
on defeating Stanley's appointment. However, they were defeated in turn by 349 to 287 votes. In protest of Stanley's
election the Dean of Norwich resigned his own position as
Select Preacher, and in his letter of resignation to the Vice-
Chancellor he remarked that

[5] *Guardian,* XXVI (Feb. 22, 1871), 218. Cited in Blackburn, *op. cit.,*
pp. 135–136.

if the pulpit of the University is to be turned into a vehicle for conveying to our youth a nerveless religion, without the bone and sinew of doctrine, a religion which can hardly be called faith so much as a mere Christianized morality, I for one must decline to stand there.[6]

Professor Blackburn has shown that Arnold took several phrases directly from the Dean of Norwich's letter and used them in *Literature and Dogma* as exemplifying the narrow dogmatic mentality against which his book was directed.

A third controversy of the period that influenced Arnold in writing *Literature and Dogma* also involved Dean Stanley. The issue had to do with the retention of the Athanasian Creed in the Book of Common Prayer. A Ritual Commission had been charged with examining the Prayer Book with regard to its directions and use. The Commission's study brought them face to face with Article 8 and the Athanasian Creed. The liberal party, led by Stanley, thought that because of the "'damnatory clauses" attached to it the use of the Athanasian Creed in services should be made optional.

Again Bishop Wilberforce led the opposition, supported by the leading Anglo-Catholic theologians E. B. Pusey and H. P. Liddon. This time the High Church party prevailed, and the Commission recommended that the Athanasian Creed be retained and that an explanatory note be appended to it making clear that "the condemnations in this Confession of Faith are to be no otherwise understood than as solemn warning of the peril of those who willfully reject the Catholic Faith." A number of the commissioners dissented from the Commission's Report and the controversy continued for almost three years. On May 7, 1873, the bishops, meeting in Convocation, issued a declaration holding that the anathemas of the Creed were in accordance with those of Holy Scripture.

[6] R. E. Prothero, *The Life and Correspondence of Arthur Penrhyn Stanley,* II, 228. Cited in Blackburn, *op. cit.*, p. 137.

Literature and Dogma was published several months before the bishops' Synodical Declaration, but Arnold was clearly aware of what direction the bishops' action would take. In the book he remarked that the Athanasian Creed "has fought and got ruffled by fighting, and is fiercely dictatorial now that it has won." Arnold had a very real dislike for the Athanasian Creed and the conception of religion that it epitomized. Whereas *Literature and Dogma* speaks disparagingly of the Nicene Creed as "learned science," it characterizes the Athanasian Creed as "learned science with a strong dash of violent and vindictive temper."

One event in particular challenged Arnold to write the articles for the *Cornhill* magazine, which in turn served as the bases for *Literature and Dogma*. On June 23, 1870, Arnold attended the formal dedication of Keble College at Oxford. The new college was named for John Keble, one of the leaders of the Oxford Movement and Matthew Arnold's own godfather. It was a time of great rejoicing among the Anglo-Catholic party, and, as it happened, the dedication occurred just at the time when the debate over the Forster Education Bill was reaching a stage of extreme agitation. Feelings on both sides were running high.

At the close of the formal dedication of the College, Lord Salisbury, the Chancellor of the University of Oxford, spoke to a public meeting on be: alf of the Keble Memorial Fund. Salisbury was a High Churchman and, apropos the occasion, addressed the following remarks to his audience:

I think this college exists to pledge us to a religion which shall not be the formless, shapeless creature of fable such as goes by the name of unsectarian religion—but shall be unsectarian in the higher sense because it is thoroughly Catholic; and that there shall be no more within these walls the idea of severing religion and dogma than there is the idea of severing the daylight from the sun.[7]

[7] *Guardian,* XXV (June 29, 1870), 762. Cited in Blackburn, *op. cit.,* p. 131.

Arnold was appalled by the speech and a few days later wrote his mother a letter that revealed both his motivation in writing *Literature and Dogma* and some of its central themes.[8] Speaking of Salisbury's address at Oxford he writes:

Religion he knows, and physical science he knows, but the immense work between the two, which is for literature to accomplish, he knows nothing of, and all his speeches at Oxford pointed this way. On the one hand, he was full of the great future for physical science, and begging the University to make up her mind to it, and to resign much of her literary studies; on the other hand, he was full, almost defiantly full, of counsels and resolves for retaining the old ecclesiastical and dogmatic form of religion. From a juxtaposition of this kind nothing but shocks and collisions can come; and I know no one, indeed, more likely to provoke shock and collisions than men like Lord Salisbury. All this pressed a good deal upon my mind at Oxford, and made me anxious, but I do hope that what influence I have may be of some use in the troubled times which I see are before us as a healing and reconciling influence, and it is this which makes me glad to find—what I find more and more—that I *have* influence.[9]

Arnold had gone to Oxford to pay homage to a leader of the Oxford Movement and to witness the dedication of a College devoted to upholding Anglo-Catholic doctrine. He came away with the idea and the stimulus for writing a book antithetical to the Anglo-Catholic conception of Christianity, a book that Arnold was later to consider his most important and that was to be more in demand than anything else he was to write.

III

In the summer and autumn of 1871, Arnold began publishing the articles that were to serve as the keynote of *Literature and Dogma*. Actually, only two articles appeared

[8] Arnold refers to Salisbury's dictum that "religion is no more to be severed from dogma than light from the sun" at least three times in *Literature and Dogma*.
[9] *Letters of Matthew Arnold 1848–88,* ed. by G. W. E. Russell (New York, 1895), II, 35. Cited in Blackburn, *op. cit.,* p. 132.

in the *Cornhill*, and the finished book was not published until February, 1873. Arnold wished to make it clear that his purpose was not to establish a bulwark against the impact of the scientific *Zeitgeist*. The scientific spirit was already having its effect in weakening traditional Christian belief, and, in Arnold's view, the time-spirit could not and should not be stayed. Neither did Arnold address himself to those who were content with the older theology or to those freethinkers who had abandoned Christianity completely. *Literature and Dogma* was written for those who

won by the modern spirit to habits of intellectual seriousness cannot receive what sets these habits at nought, and will not try to force themselves to do so, but who have stood near enough to the Christian religion to feel the attraction which a thing so very great, when one stands really near to it, cannot but exercize, and who have some familiarity with the Bible and some practice in using it.

Arnold believed that those who felt both the irresistible character of the *Zeitgeist* and the incomparable greatness of Biblical religion must now seek to place the truth of that religion on "a new experimental basis." For Arnold, that meant establishing the truths of Christianity on the unassailable ground of human experience. The preliminary step to such a reconception of Christianity involved recognition of the fact that the language of the Bible is not to be confused with the language of science. Biblical language is not "rigid and fixed," but "fluid, passing, literary"; it is language "thrown out," as Arnold was so often to remark. It is a language of image and metaphor, symbol and myth. To appreciate the true character of the biblical literature one needs the help not of science and metaphysics, but of culture—of literary taste that alone can save the reader from an indiscriminate literalizing of everything he reads. Only a broad acquaintance with culture will, in Arnold's opinion, spare men from the philistine pretension of equating truth with scientific statement.

If this preliminary step is observed, one will go to the Bible and discover that the ancient Hebrews had no intention of being read as scientists or metaphysicians. For them God was not the conclusion of a rational inference. What the Israelites did discover, and passed on to us as a matchless heritage, was the experience that *"Righteousness tendeth to life."* "No people ever felt so strongly that succeeding, going right, hitting the mark in this great concern, was *the way of peace*, the highest possible satisfaction." This eternal law of righteousness the Israelites experienced as a power not of their own making, which they personified as God. However, the God of the ancient Hebrews, whom Arnold called "the Eternal not ourselves which makes for righteousness," was not the God of the Bishops of Gloucester and Winchester; i.e., a metaphysical doctrine. The "Eternal not ourselves" was attested to and verified by the inescapable experience of the moral life: that the eternal law of righteousness tendeth to life, to happiness, and to peace.

In time Israel lost sight of this original perception. The Israelites began to look not to the law of righteousness but to supernatural, miraculous intervention as their only hope of salvation. Hence, to its sublime insight Israel proceeded to add *Aberglaube,* or "extra-beliefs," * particularly those speculative eschatological prophecies of a future Messiah. Belief was no longer grounded in certain experience. Israel's faith became other-worldly and miraculous. What was needed once more was a restoration of the personal and experiential—religion newly imbued with deep feeling, inwardness, and authenticity. This was what Jesus provided.

Jesus accomplished this renewal by a "method" of inwardness (*metanoia*, repentance, change of heart) and a "secret" of self-renouncement (*necrosis*, dying to the old self), which he combined with his unique mildness and "sweet-reasonableness." By this method and secret, Jesus

* Arnold was fond of rendering the German word *Aberglaube* as "extra-belief." *Aberglaube* is usually translated as "superstition."

"made his followers feel that in these qualities lay the secret of their best self; that to attain them was in the highest degree requisite and natural, and that a man's whole happiness depended on it."

However, once again spiritual truth was overladen with a "materializing mythology," with popular *Aberglaube*. Jesus's own disciples did not understand him. He was too far above them. Jesus, it is true, used the popular mythology of his day, but in *a spiritual sense*. However, his meaning was lost on his followers, and they portrayed him as a thaumaturgist and apocalyptical visionary. And with the passing of time Christianity fixed more and more on these purely miraculous and futuristic elements in the Gospels. Christianity no longer rested on its natural truth, that righteousness makes for life and for peace, but on the proofs of prophecy and miracle.

Even greater place was given to the miraculous and the metaphysical as Christianity spread through the Hellenistic world. Finally these "extra-beliefs" were formalized and reduced to scientific exactitude in the Apostles' and Nicene Creeds—the "popular" and "learned" sciences of Christianity. The distance traveled from the Bible to these Creeds was very great, and the dogmatizing process has left us with beliefs that are neither sure nor verifiable. It has foisted upon us "extra-beliefs" that were falsely constructed "by taking certain great names and great promises too literally and materially."

Thus has Christianity remained to Arnold's day—its truth defended on the tenuous ground of *Aberglaube*. But, says Arnold,

there is always a drawback to a man's advantage in . . . treating, in religion and conduct, what is extra-belief, and not certain, as if it were matter of certaintly, and in making it his ground of action —*he pays for it*. The time comes when he discovers that it is *not* certain; and then the whole certainty of religion seems discredited, and the basis of conduct gone.

Arnold believed that Christianity was now "paying" for its false proofs from miracle and prophecy and its dogmatizing by seeing the Bible and its incomparable truths increasingly discredited in the minds of the people. What had happened is that religion was

made to stand on its apex instead of on its base; righteousness supported on ecclesiastical dogma, instead of ecclesiastical dogma being supported on righteousness.

Arnold considered the loss of the Bible's influence on the people as tragic, for he viewed the secular alternatives of Spencer, Comte, Bradlaugh, and Leslie Stephen as either fatuous nonsense or unctuous truism when compared with the sublimity and the morally transforming power of the biblical literature. What Arnold called for was a reading of the Bible anew in its original, natural light—as our most valuable poetry of life. So read, the Bible would no longer be viewed as "prescientific error" but as that which must remain as the indispensible supplement to our scientific work—without which our lives would become flat and brutish, lacking all spiritual grace or vision.

IV

Despite the fact that it was written a century ago, Arnold's unorthodox defense of the Bible and Christianity in *Literature and Dogma* has a very contemporary ring to it. What Arnold was calling for then has certain parallels with developments in the radical and secular Christian theologies of recent years. The similarity between Arnold's program and contemporary theology is especially striking in relation to: 1) the "demythologization" of the Bible, called for by the German theologian Rudolf Bultmann, and 2) the reduction of theological language to its conative or moral use, as proposed in recent years by several British and American analytical philosophers.

Matthew Arnold did not use the term "myth" in the

technical sense in which it is used today by theologians and historians of religion. Nevertheless, what he called *Aberglaube*, or "extra-belief," is similar to what Bultmann and other theologians now call myth. Arnold was as acutely conscious then as Bultmann is today of the problem Christianity faces in grounding its truth in the message of the Bible—a message that is couched in a language and a world view that are alien and unacceptable to a modern, scientific age. Bultmann has summarized the nature and problem of biblical *Aberglaube* in the following classic passage:

The cosmology of the New Testament is essentially mythical in character. The world is a three-storied structure, with the earth in the center, the heaven above, and the underworld beneath. Heaven is the abode of God and of celestial beings—the angels. The underworld is hell, the place of torment. Even the earth is more than the scene of natural, everyday events. . . . It is the scene of the supernatural activity of God and his angels on the one hand and of Satan and his daemons on the other. . . . This aeon is held in bondage by Satan, sin, and death (for "powers" is precisely what they are) and hastens toward its end. That end will come very soon, and will take the form of a cosmic catastrophe. It will be inaugurated by the woes of the last time. Then the judge will come from heaven, the dead will rise, the last judgment will take place, and men will enter into eternal salvation or damnation.

This then is the mythical view of the world which the New Testament presupposes when it presents the event of redemption which is the subject of its preaching. It proclaims in the language of mythology that the last time has now come. "In the fullness of time" God sent forth his Son, a pre-existent divine Being, who appears on earth as a man. He dies the death of a sinner on the cross and makes atonement for the sins of men. His resurrection marks the beginning of the cosmic catastrophe. Death, the consequence of Adam's sin, is abolished. . . . The risen Christ is exalted to the right hand of God in heaven, and made "Lord" and "King." He will come again on the clouds of heaven to complete the work of redemption and the resurrection and judgment of men will follow. . . .

All this is the language of mythology, and the origin of the various themes can be easily traced in the contemporary mythology of Jewish Apocalyptic and in the redemption myths of Gnosticism. To this extent the kerygma (proclamation) is incredible to modern man, for he is convinced that the mythical view of the world is obsolete. We are therefore bound to ask whether, when we preach the Gospel today, we expect our converts to accept not only the Gospel message, but also the mythical view of the world in which it is set. If not, does the New Testament embody a truth which is quite independent of its mythical setting? If it does, theology must understand the task of stripping the kerygma from its mythical framework, of "demythologizing" it.[10]

In *Literature and Dogma* Arnold distinguishes clearly between the apocalyptical and dogmatical *Aberglaube* of primitive Christianity and what he considers the "true essence" of the religion of Israel and of Jesus and calls for a "demythologizing" of the *Aberglaube*. Arnold and Bultmann, each in his own terms, appeal for a recasting of the essential Christian message in language consonant with the experience of modern men. In both cases what this requires is a *reinterpretation* of the ancient Christian *mythos*.

Neither Arnold nor Bultmann wish to reject the mythological *Aberglaube* of the Bible. They both recognize myth as an indispensable form of religious expression. Arnold referred to *Aberglaube* as "the poetry of life," and he was certain that man could not live without his poetic myths. He asserted:

For the popular science (*Aberglaube*) of religion, one has, or ought to have, an infinite tenderness. It is the spontaneous work of nature. It is the travail of the human mind to adapt to its grasp and employment great ideas of which it feels the attraction, but for which, except as given to it by this travail, it would have been immature. . . . To call it, as many of our philosophical

[10] Rudolf Bultmann, "New Testament and Mythology," in *Kerygma and Myth,* I, ed. by Hans Werner Bartsch (London, 1953), 1–3.

Liberal friends are fond of calling it, "a degrading superstition," is as untrue, as it is poor compliment to human nature.

Speaking of the great eschatological myths of Israel and primitive Christianity Arnold wrote: "Now, most of this has a poetical value, some of it has a moral value. All of it is, in truth, *a testimony to the strength of Israel's idea of right-eousness.*" This last sentence is the clue to Arnold's under-standing of the function of religious myth and his demand for reinterpretation. Or, as Bultmann has expressed it: "The real purpose of myth is not to present an objective picture of the world as it is, but to express man's under-standing of himself in the world in which he lives. Myth should be interpreted not cosmologically, but anthropolog-ically, or better existentially." [11]

The task of demythologization is to reinterpret the bib-lical mythology so that the essential message of the Bible can be understood for what it is and not be confused with an outdated world-view. Demythologization demands that the moral or existential intention of the myth be identified and restated in non-mythological terms. For Arnold, myth is the poetic representation of man's experience of relation-ship to God, or what, in more scientific language, Arnold termed "the stream of tendency by which all things seek to fulfill the law of their being." The law of man's being is righteousness, and it was axiomatic to Arnold that "right-eousness tendeth to life." And when men are deeply atten-tive to the moral life, one thing cannot fail to strike them, viz., "the very great part in righteousness which belongs, we may say, to *not ourselves.*"

Arnold believed that we must, in truth, say with Thomas à Kempis: "Left to ourselves, we sink and perish; visited, we lift up our heads and live." But we can speak of our dependence and of our self-surrender to that by which we are graced or "visited" only in the language of poetry and myth—not in the language of science. Myth and poetry

[11] *Ibid.,* p. 10.

alone can give wing to the faith and hopes and aspirations of men's spirits; they alone can integrate the personality around some great loyalty, fire the will, and liberate the spirit of man from the blind contingency of nature.

For Arnold, myth was indispensable. But what is needed is that its meaning and use be properly identified and communicated. Myth is the means by which a people represent imaginatively their own moral understanding of existence. And such symbolic renderings of our moral faith lie in a dimension outside the circle of scientific verification and will always remain a necessary complement to scientific endeavor. As Arnold expressed it:

Poetry gives the idea but it gives it touched with beauty, heightened by emotion. . . . Science . . . adds thought to thought, accumulates the elements of a synthesis which will never be complete until it is touched with beauty and emotion; and when it is touched with these, it has passed out of the sphere of science.[12]

The first step, then, in properly interpreting the Bible is to understand that biblical language is essentially mythopoetic.

This brings us to the second point of comparison between Arnold and contemporary theology; viz., the corresponding appeal to the moral or conative use of religious language. Arnold's distinction between "Literature" and "Dogma" is analogous to the distinction made nowadays by linguistic analysts between *conative* and *scientific* language. A major contribution to this distinction was made recently by R. B. Braithwaite in *An Empiricist's View of the Nature of Religious Belief*. Braithwaite agrees with Arnold that while religious statements are empirical, they are not assertions that can be verified by a *hard* scientific test. Nevertheless, this does not mean, as the scientific positivist would have it, that religious statements are meaningless or useless.

[12] *Essays, Letters and Reviews by Matthew Arnold*, ed. by Fraser Neiman (Cambridge, 1960), p. 238.

Following Wittgenstein, Braithwaite argues that the *meaning* of a word or statement is to be found in its use, not in its verification.

How, then, is the use of religious language to be understood by someone like Arnold, who wants religious statements to reflect real experience—to be straightforwardly and radically empirical—without requiring a hard scientific proof? Braithwaite answers that to fulfill this demand religious assertions must be seen as serving a moral or conative use. So understood, religious statements need not claim to be factual assertions, but neither should they be considered merely "emotive" expressions. Moral assertions function as the expression of an intention to act in certain ways. They are conative rather than simply emotive. "Just as the meaning of a moral assertion is given by its use in expressing the asserter's intention to act, so far as in him lies, in accordance with the moral principle involved, so the meaning of a religious assertion is given by its use in expressing the asserter's intention to follow a specified policy of behavior." [13]

However, religious language not only indicates an intention to act in a certain way; it also serves a second, morally supportive function: that is, religious assertions have an element in them lacking in purely moral assertions in that they refer to a *story* that is integral to the intention. What Braithwaite calls a story, "Matthew Arnold called a *parable* and a *fairy-tale*." [14] And, according to Braithwaite, "a man is not a professsing Christian unless he both proposes to live according to Christian moral principles *and* associates his intention with thinking Christian stories; but he need not believe that the empirical propositions presented by the stories correspond to empirical fact." [15]

What religious stories, parables, or myths *do* is to give psychological impetus to the will and strength to persevere

[13]R. B. Braithwaite, *An Empiricist's View of the Nature of Religious Belief* (Cambridge, 1955), p. 16.
[14] *Ibid.*, p. 27.   [15] *Ibid.*

in carrying out one's moral intentions in the face of weakness and temptation. What distinguishes the several religions is their stories, which connote different policies of action. It follows that commitment to the *right* religious stories is of the greatest importance, inasmuch as the choice of stories has enormous moral consequences. While it is immaterial whether or not the stories are based on factual history or are purely fictitious, they do produce results that are experientially testable. For this reason, religious literature is to be taken with the utmost seriousness as the principal guide and impetus to the moral life of men and societies.

To Arnold, the language of the Bible functions in the same conative way as pseudo-statement, i.e., as statements "justified entirely by [their] effects in releasing or organizing our impulses and attitudes." [16] Thus Arnold can assert that since the object of religion is conduct, "if a man helps himself in his conduct by taking an object of hope and presentiment as if it were an object of certainty he may even be said to gain thereby an advantage." The truth and value of an assertion lies in its moral fruits, in what Arnold called its "experimental" test. All religious statements can be translated into their moral equivalents. However, religious language is far more satisfying, for the reason that religion is morality touched by the indispensable ingredient of emotion. Take, for example, the language about God:

God or the *Eternal* is here really, at bottom, nothing but a deeply moved way of saying "the power that makes for *conduct* or *righteousness*." "Trust in *God*" is, in a deeply moved way of expression, the trust in the law of conduct; "delight in the Eternal" is, in a deeply moved way of expression, the happiness we all feel to spring from conduct. . . . Attending to conduct, to judgment, makes the attender feel that it is joy to do it. Attending to it more still, makes him feel that it is the commandment of the Eternal, and that the joy got from it is joy got from

[16] I. A. Richards, "Science and Poetry," in *Criticism,* ed. by Mark Schorer, *et al.* (New York, 1948), p. 518.

fulfilling the commandment of the Eternal. . . . "The fear of the Eternal, that is wisdom; and to depart from evil, that is understanding" (Job 28: 28) : *"The fear of the Eternal"* and *"To depart from evil"* here mean, and are put to mean, and by the very laws of Hebrew composition which make the second phrase in a parallelism repeat the first in other words, they *must* mean, just the same thing. Yet what man of soul, after he had once risen to feel that to depart from evil was to walk in awful observance of an enduring clue, within us and without us, which leads to happiness, but would prefer to say, instead of "to depart from evil," the fear of the Eternal? Henceforth, then, Israel transferred to this Eternal all his obligations. Instead of saying "Whosoever keepeth the commandments keepeth his own soul" he rather said, "My soul, wait thou only upon *God,* for of him cometh my salvation! . . ." That is, with Israel *religion* replaced morality.

What Arnold has in common with many of the contemporary radical theologians is the conviction that being a Christian and being a modern man are not mutually exclusive. The *Zeitgeist* cannot be denied, and this demands that we accept an empirical or secular attitude and interpret Christianity in terms of the modern empirical temper. While biblical language about God may be noncognitive in the strict sense, such language does permit a kind of verification; i.e., whether such affirmations do, in fact, issue in a certain pattern of action, a certain attitude about life and its duties.[17] This for Arnold, and for the secular theologian today, is what really matters in Christianity and not the precise metaphysical definitions of the dogmatists.

Whether Christianity could long remain a living faith without grounding its affirmations about the world and human action in some metaphysical claims (i.e., dogmas) about the nature of reality is questionable. Arnold, on the contrary, was confident that Christianity would command the allegiance of people *only* if it freed itself of its meta-

[17] Note, as another example, the similarity between Arnold's program and that of Paul Van Buren in *The Secular Meaning of the Gospel* (New York, 1963).

physical pretensions. For Arnold, the essence of Christianity is to be found in Jesus's sublime secret: "The word of the cross or *necrosis*, 'dying.' Jesus taught that there are in every man two lives: the life of the old self—the life of bondage to the world and the flesh—and what he called *life, real life, eternal life*. And Jesus's secret is that only in renouncing, in dying to the old self, will a man live—that is, that *the word of the cross* is in fact *the word of the Kingdom*. Jesus, above everyone, saw that in the cross was genuine *peace, joy, life*. For Arnold, that is what Christianity is all about.

Selected Bibliography

I. Works on religion by Matthew Arnold

   A. Books:

      St. Paul and Protestantism, 1870
      Literature and Dogma, 1873
      God and the Bible, 1875
      Last Essays on Church and Religion, 1877

   B. Essays:

      "The Bishop and the Philosopher," 1863
      "Dr. Stanley's Lectures on the Jewish Church," 1863
      "Spinoza and the Bible," 1865
      "A First Requisite of Church Reform," 1870

For the latest, critical editions of Arnold's prose works on religion, the reader is referred to *The Complete Prose Works of Matthew Arnold*, Vols. 1–6, ed. by R. H. Super (Ann Arbor: The University of Michigan Press, 1960–68), and *Essays, Letters and Reviews by Matthew Arnold*, ed. by Fraser Neiman (Cambridge: Harvard University Press, 1960).

II. Works about *Literature and Dogma* and Matthew Arnold as critic of religion.

   Blackburn, William. *Matthew Arnold's Literature and Dogma*. Ph. D. dissertation. Yale University, 1943.

      A thorough study of the text and the immediate and larger background of *Literature and Dogma*.

See also: William Blackburn. "The Background of Arnold's *Literature and Dogma.*" *Modern Philology.* XLIII (November, 1945), 133.

Cockshut, A. O. J. "Matthew Arnold: Conservative Revolutionary." *The Unbelievers.* London: Collins, 1964.

Robbins, William. *The Ethical Idealism of Matthew Arnold.* London: William Heinemann, Ltd., 1959.

A sympathetic study of the sources of Arnold's religious ideas and their place in the religious situation of Arnold's day and our own.

Super, R. H., ed. *The Complete Prose Works of Matthew Arnold.* Vol. VI: *Dissent and Dogma.* Ann Arbor: The University of Michigan Press, 1968.

Dissent and Dogma contains a new, critical edition of *Literature and Dogma.* Super's critical and explanatory notes to the text are invaluable.

Trilling, Lionel. *Matthew Arnold.* New York: W. W. Norton and Company, 1939.

Trilling's book is still widely considered the best study of Arnold as Victorian poet, social, and religious critic.

Willey, Basil. "Matthew Arnold." *Nineteenth Century Studies.* New York: Harper Torchbooks, 1966.

This is a perceptive and appreciative essay on Arnold as a religious writer.

Note
about the Text

This abridged edition of *Literature and Dogma* is based on the Popular Edition of 1883. Arnold's quotations from ancient and modern authors in the original foreign language have been deleted from the footnotes. Arnold's citations of biblical texts remain. Chapter subheadings are those of the editor, as are several footnotes, which are so indicated.

J. C. L.

Contents

Contents

Preface
To the Popular Edition
(1883)

Reason for a popular edition

. . . I do not choose for the experiment of a popular edition this book, merely because it admits of being shortened, or because it has been much in demand. I choose it far more for the reason that I think it, of all my books in prose, the one most important (if I may say so) and most capable of being useful. Ten years ago, when it was first published, I explained my design in writing it. No one who has had experience of the inattention and random judgments of mankind will be very quick to cry out because a serious design is not fairly and fully apprehended. *Literature and Dogma*, however, has perhaps had more than its due share of misrepresentation.

The sole notion of *Literature and Dogma*, with many people, is that it is a book containing an abominable illustration, and attacking Christianity. . . . Let me add a word or two as to the notion that *Literature and Dogma* is an attack upon Christianity. It is not even an attack upon the errors of popular Christianity. Those errors are very open to attack; they are much attacked already, and in a fashion, often, which I dislike and condemn; they will certainly be attacked more and more, until they perish. But it is not the object of *Literature and Dogma* to attack them. Neither, on the other hand, is it the object of *Literature and Dogma* to contend with the enemies and deniers of Christianity, and to convince them of their error. Sooner or later, indeed, they will be convinced of it, but by other agencies

1

and through a quite other force than mine; it is not the object of *Literature and Dogma* to confute them.

The object of *Literature and Dogma* is to re-assure those who feel attachment to Christianity, to the Bible, but who recognise the growing discredit befalling miracles and the supernatural. Such persons are to be re-assured, not by disguising or extenuating the discredit which has befallen miracles and the supernatural, but by insisting on the natural truth of Christianity. That miracles have fallen into discredit is to be frankly admitted; that they have fallen into discredit justly and necessarily, and through the very same natural and salutary process which had previously extinguished our belief in witchcraft, is to be frankly admitted also. Even ten years ago, when *Literature and Dogma* was first published, lucidity on this matter was, on the whole, not dangerous but expedient; it is even yet more expedient to-day. It has become even yet more manifest that by the sanction of miracles Christianity can no longer stand; it can stand only by its natural truth.

Natural truth of Christianity, not miraculous sanctions, real concern of this book

Of course, to pass from Christianity relying on its miracles to a Christianity relying on its natural truth is a great change. It can only be brought about by those whose attachment to Christianity is such, that they cannot part with it, and yet cannot but deal with it sincerely. This was the case with the Germanic nations who brought about that former great change, the Reformation. Probably the abandonment of the tie with Rome was hardly less of a change to the Christendom of the sixteenth century, than the abandonment of the proof from miracles is to the Christendom of to-day. Yet the Germanic nations broke the tie with Rome, because they loved Christianity well enough to deal sincerely with themselves as to clericalism and tradition. The Latin nations did not break their tie with Rome. This was not because they loved Rome more, or because they less saw the truth as to clericalism or tradition—a truth which had become evident enough then, as the truth about miracles has become now. But they did not really care enough about Christianity (I speak of the nations, not, of course, of individuals) to feel compelled to deal sincerely with themselves about it. The heretical Germanic nations, who renounced clericalism and tradition, proved their attachment to Christianity by so doing, and preserved for it that serious hold upon men's minds which is a great and beneficent force to-day, and the force to which *Literature and Dogma* makes appeal. Miracles have to go the same way as clericalism and tradition; and the important thing is, not that the world should be acute enough to see this (there needs, indeed, no remarkable acuteness to see it), but that a great and progressive part of the world should be capable of seeing this and of yet holding fast to Christianity.

To assist those called to such an endeavour, is the object, I repeat, of *Literature and Dogma*. It is not an attack upon miracles and the supernatural. It unreservedly admits, indeed, that the belief in them has given way and cannot be restored, it recommends entire lucidity of mind on this subject, it points out certain characters of weakness in the sanction drawn from miracles, even while the belief in them lasted. Its real concern, however, is not with miracles, but with the natural truth of Christianity. It is after this that, among the more serious races of the world, the hearts of men are really feeling; and what really furthers them is to establish it. At present, reformers in religion are far too negative, spending their labour, some of them, in inveighing against false beliefs which are doomed, others, in contending about matters of discipline and ritual which are indifferent. Popular Christianity derived its power from the characters of certainty and of grandeur which it wore; these characters do actually belong to Christianity in its natural truth, and to show them there should be our object. This alone is really important. . . .

Preface
(1873)

An inevitable revolution, of which we all recognise the beginnings and signs, but which has already spread, perhaps, farther than most of us think, is befalling the religion in which we have been brought up. In those countries where religion has been most loved, this revolution will be felt the most keenly; felt through all its stages and in all its incidents. In no country will it be more felt than in England. This cannot be otherwise. It cannot be but that the revolution should come, and that it should be here felt passionately, profoundly, painfully. In regard to it, however, there is incumbent on every one the utmost duty of considerateness and caution. There can be no surer proof of a narrow and ill-instructed mind, than to think and uphold that what a man takes to be the truth on religious matters is always to be proclaimed. Our truth on these matters, and likewise the error of others, is something so relative, that the good or harm likely to be done by speaking ought always to be taken into account. "I keep silence at many things," says Goethe, "for I would not mislead men, and am well content if others can find satisfaction in what gives me offence." The man who believes that his truth on religious matters is so absolutely the truth, that say it when, and where, and to whom he will, he cannot but do good with it, is in our day almost always a man whose truth is half blunder, and wholly useless.

To be convinced, therefore, that our current theology is false, is not necessarily a reason for publishing that conviction. The theology may be false, and yet one may do more harm in attacking it than by keeping silence and waiting. To judge rightly the time and its conditions is the great thing; there is a time, as the Preacher says, to speak, and a time to keep silence. If the present time is a time to speak, there must be a reason why it is so.

Rejection of the Bible by the masses

And there *is* a reason; and it is this. Clergymen and ministers of religion are full of lamentations over what they call the spread of scepticism, and because of the little hold which religion now has on the masses of the people—the *lapsed masses*, as some call them. Practical hold on them it never, perhaps, had very much, but they did not question its truth, and they held it in considerable awe. As the best of them raised themselves up out of a merely animal life, religion attracted and engaged them. But now they seem to have hardly any awe of it at all, and they freely question its truth. And many of the most successful, energetic, and ingenious of the artisan class, who are steady and wise, are now found either of themselves rejecting the Bible altogether, or following teachers who tell them that the Bible is an exploded superstition. Let me quote from the letter of a workingman—a man, himself, of no common intelligence and temper—a passage that sets this forth very clearly. "Despite the efforts of the churches," he says, "the speculations of the day are working their way down among the people, many of whom are asking for the *reason* and *authority* for the things they have been taught to believe. Questions of this kind, too, mostly reach them through doubtful channels; and owing to this, and to their lack of culture, a discovery of imperfection and fallibility in the Bible leads to its contemptuous rejection as a great priestly imposture. And thus those among the working class who eschew the teachings of the orthodox, slide off towards, not the late Mr. Maurice,* nor yet Professor Huxley, but towards Mr. Bradlaugh."

---

* F. D. Maurice (1805–72) was the outstanding Anglican theologian of mid-Victorian England. T. H. Huxley (1825–1895),

Despite the efforts of the churches, the writer tells us, this contemptuous rejection of the Bible happens. And we regret the rejection as much as the clergy and ministers of religion do. There may be others who do not regret it, but we do. All that the churches can say about the importance of the Bible and its religion, we concur in. And it is the religion of the Bible that is professedly in question with all the churches, when they talk of religion and lament its prospects. With Catholics as well as Protestants, and with all the sects of Protestantism, this is so: and from the nature of the case it must be so. What the religion of the Bible is, how it is to be got at, they may not agree; but that it is the religion of the Bible for which they contend, they all aver. "The Bible," says Cardinal Newman, "is the record of the whole revealed faith; so far all parties agree." Now, this religion of the Bible we say they cannot value more than we do. If we hesitate to adopt strictly their language about its *all*-importance, that is only because we take an uncommonly large view of human perfection, and say, speaking strictly, that there go to this certain things—art, for instance, and science —which the Bible hardly meddles with. The difference between us and them, however, is more a difference of theoretical statement than of practical conclusion. Speaking practically, and looking at the very large part of human life engaged by the Bible, at the comparatively small part unengaged by it, we are quite willing, like the churches, to call the Bible and its religion *all*-important.

Cause of neglect of the Bible: its unverifiable base

All this agreement there is, both in words and in things, between us and the churches. And yet, when we behold the clergy and ministers of religion lament the neglect of religion and aspire to restore it, how must we feel that to

natural scientist and defender of Darwin, was a leading agnostic. Charles Bradlaugh (1833–91) was one of the most militant free-thinkers of his day.—*Ed.*

restore religion as they understand it, to re-inthrone the
Bible as explained by our current theology, whether learned
or popular, is absolutely and for ever impossible!—as impossible as to restore the feudal system, or the belief in witches.
Let us admit that the Bible cannot possibly die; but then
the churches cannot even conceive the Bible without the
gloss which they at present put upon it, and this gloss, as
certainly, cannot possibly live. And it is not a gloss which
one church or one sect puts upon the Bible and another
does not; it is the gloss they *all* put upon it, calling it the
substratum of belief common to all Christian churches, and
largely shared with them even by natural religion. It is this
so-called axiomatic basis which must go, and it supports all
the rest. If the Bible were really inseparable from this and
depended upon it, then Mr. Bradlaugh would have his way
and the Bible would go too; since this basis is inevitably
doomed. For whatever is to stand must rest upon something
which is verifiable, not unverifiable. Now, the assumption
with which all the churches and sects set out, that there is "a
Great Personal First Cause, the moral and intelligent Governor of the universe," and that from him the Bible derives
its authority, cannot at present, at any rate, be verified.

Those who "ask for the *reason* and *authority* for the
things they have been taught to believe," as the people, we
are told, are now doing, will begin at the beginning. Rude
and hard reasoners as they are, they will never consent to
admit, as a self-evident axiom, the preliminary assumption
with which the churches start. But this preliminary assumption governs everything which in our current theology follows it; and it is certain, therefore, that the people will not
receive our current theology. So, if they are to receive the
Bible, we must find for the Bible some other basis than that
which the churches assign to it, a verifiable basis and not an
assumption; and this, again, will govern everything which
comes after. This new religion of the Bible the people may
receive; the version now current of the religion of the Bible
they never will receive.

Here, then, is the problem: to find, for the Bible, for Christianity, for our religion, a basis in something which can be verified, instead of in something which has to be assumed. . . . With this unsolved, all other religious discussion is idle trifling. . . .

Culture necessary for a proper understanding of the Bible

There is now an end to all fear of doing harm by gainsaying the received theology of the churches and sects. For this theology is itself now a hindrance to the Bible rather than a help. Nay, to abandon it, to put some other construction on the Bible than this theology puts, to find some other basis for the Bible than this theology finds, is indispensable, if we would have the Bible reach the people. And this is the aim of the following essay: to show that, when we come to put the right construction on the Bible, we give to the Bible a real experimental basis, and keep on this basis throughout; instead of any basis of unverifiable assumption to start with, followed by a string of other unverifiable assumptions of the like kind, such as the received theology necessitates.

And this aim we cannot seek without coming in sight of another aim too, which we have often and often pointed out, and tried to recommend: *culture*, the acquainting ourselves with the best that has been known and said in the world, and thus with the history of the human spirit. One cannot go far in the attempt to bring in, for the Bible, a right construction, without seeing how necessary is something of culture to its being admitted and used. The correspondent whom we have above quoted notices how the lack of culture disposes the masses to conclude at once, from any imperfection or fallibility in the Bible, that it is a priestly imposture. To a certain extent this is the fault, not of the people's want of culture, but of the priests and theologians themselves, who for centuries have kept assuring men that perfect and infallible the Bible is. Still, even without this confusion added by his theological instructors, the *homo unius libri*, the man of no range in his reading, must almost inevitably misunderstand the Bible, cannot treat it largely enough, must be inclined to treat it all alike, and to press every word.

For, on the one hand, he has not enough experience of the way in which men have thought and spoken, to feel what the Bible-writers are about; to read between the lines, to discern where he ought to rest with his whole weight, and where he ought to pass lightly. On the other hand, the void and hunger in his mind, from want of ailment, almost irresistibly impels him to fill it by taking literally, and amplifying, certain data which he finds in the Bible, whether they ought to be so dealt with or no. Our mechanical and materializing theology, with its insane licence of affirmation about God, its insane licence of affirmation about a future state, is really the result of the poverty and inanition of our minds. It is because we cannot trace God in history that we stay the craving of our minds with a fancy-account of him, made up by putting scattered expressions of the Bible together, and taking them literally; it is because we have such a scanty sense of the life of humanity, that we proceed in the like manner in our scheme of a future state. He that cannot watch the God of the Bible, and the salvation of the Bible, gradually and on an immense scale discovering themselves and *becoming*, will insist on seeing them ready-made, and in such precise and reduced dimensions as may suit his narrow mind.

To understand that the language of the Bible is fluid, passing, and literary, not rigid, fixed, and scientific, is the first step towards a right understanding of the Bible. But to take this very first step, some experience of how men have thought and expressed themselves, and some flexibility of spirit, are necessary. . . . And thus we come back to our old remedy of *culture*—knowing the best that has been thought and known in the world; which turns out to be, in another shape, and in particular relation to the Bible, *getting the power, through reading, to estimate the proportion and relation in what we read.* If we read but a very little, we naturally want to press it all; if we read a great deal, we are willing not to press the whole of what we read, and we learn what ought to be pressed and what not. Now this is really the very foundation of any sane criticism. . . .

We can hardly urge this topic too much, of so great a practical importance is it, and above all at the present time. To be able to control what one reads by means of the discriminative tact coming, in a clear and fair mind, from a wide experience, was never perhaps so necessary as in the England of our own day, and in theology, and in what concerns the Bible itself. And to our popular religion it is especially difficult; because we have been trained to regard the Bible, not as a book whose parts have varying degrees of value, but as the Jews came to regard their Scriptures, as a sort of talisman given down to us out of Heaven, with all its parts equipollent. And yet there was a time when Jews knew well the vast difference there is between books like Esther, Chronicles, or Daniel, and books like Genesis or Isaiah. There was a time when Christians knew well the vast difference between the First Epistle of Peter and his so-called Second Epistle, or between the Epistle to the Hebrews and the Epistles to the Romans and to the Corinthians. This indeed, is what makes the religious watchword of the British and Foreign School Society: *The Bible, the whole Bible and nothing but the Bible!* so ingeniously (one must say) absurd; it is treating the Bible as Mahometans treat the Koran, as if it were a talisman all of one piece, and with all its sentences equipollent.

Not all books of the Bible are to be taken equally

Yet the very expressions, *Canon of Scripture, Canonical Books,* recall a time when degrees of value were still felt, and all parts of the Bible did not stand on the same footing, and were not taken equally. There was a time when books were read as part of the Bible which are in no Bible now; there was a time when books which are in every Bible now, were by many disallowed as genuine parts of the Bible. St.

Athanasius rejected the Book of Esther, and the Greek Christianity of the East repelled the Apocalypse, and the Latin Christianity of the West repelled the Epistle to the Hebrews. And a true critical sense of relative value lay at the bottom of all these rejections. No one rejected Isaiah or the Epistle to the Romans. The books rejected were such books as those which we now print as the Apocrypha, or as the Book of Esther, or the Epistle to the Hebrews, or the so-called Epistle of Jude, or the so-called Second Epistle of St. Peter, or the two short Epistles following the main Epistle attributed to St. John, or the Apocalypse.

Now, whatever value one may assign to these works, no sound critic would rate their intrinsic worth as high as that of the great undisputed books of the Bible. And so far from their finally getting where they now are after a thorough trial of their claims, and with indisputable propriety, they got placed there by the force of circumstances, by chance or by routine, rather than on their merits. Indeed, by merit alone the Book of Esther could have no right at all to be now in our Canon while Ecclesiasticus is not, nor the Epistle of Jude and the Second Epistle of Peter rather than the First Epistle of Clement. But the whole discussion died out, not because the matter was sifted and settled and a perfect Canon of Scripture deliberately formed; it died out as medieval ignorance deepened, and because there was no longer knowledge or criticism enough left in the world to keep such a discussion alive.

And so things went on till the Renascence, when criticism came to life again. But the Church had now long since adopted the Vulgate, and her authority was concerned in maintaining what she had adopted. Luther and Calvin, on the other hand, recurred to the old true notion of a difference in rank and genuineness among the Bible books. For they both of them insisted on the criterion of internal evidence for Scripture: "the witness of the Spirit." How freely Luther used this criterion, we may see by reading in the old editions of his Bible his prefaces, which in succeeding editions have long ceased to appear. Whether he used it aright we will not now inquire, but he used it freely. Taunted, however, by Rome with their divisions, their want of a fixed authority like the Church, Protestants were driven to make the Bible this fixed authority; and so the Bible came to be regarded as a thing all of a piece, endued with talismanic virtues. It came to be regarded as something different from anything it had originally ever been, or primitive times had ever imagined it to be. And Protestants did practically in this way use the Bible more irrationally than Rome practically ever used it; for Rome had her hypothesis of the Church Catholic endued with talismanic virtues, and did not want a talismanic Bible too. All this perversion has made a discriminating use of the Bible-documents very difficult in our country; yet without it a sound criticism of the Bible is impossible. . . .

But to return. Difficult, certainly, is the right reading of the Bible, and true culture, too, is difficult. For true culture implies not only knowledge, but right tact and justness of judgement, forming themselves by and with knowledge; without this tact, it is not true culture. Difficult, however, as true culture is, it is necessary. For, after all, the Bible is *not* a talisman, to be taken and used literally; neither is any existing Church a talisman, whatever pretensions of the sort it may make, for giving the right interpretation of the Bible. Only true culture can give us this interpretation; so that if conduct is, as it is, inextricably bound up with the Bible and the right interpretation of it, then the importance of culture becomes unspeakable. For if conduct is necessary (and there is nothing so necessary), culture is necessary.

Introduction

1

The despisers of letters

Lord Beaconsfield,* treating Hellenic things with the scornful negligence natural to a Hebrew, said in a well-known book that our aristocratic class, the polite flower of the nation, were truly Hellenic in this respect among others —that they cared nothing for letters and never read. Now, there seems to be here some inaccuracy, if we take our standard of what is Hellenic from Hellas at its highest pitch of development. . . . But no doubt Lord Beaconsfield was thinking of the primitive Hellenes of northwestern Greece, from among whom the Dorians of Peloponnesus originally came, but who themselves remained in their old seats and did not migrate and develop like their more famous brethren. And of these primitive Hellenes, of Greeks like the Chaonians and Molossians, it is probably a very just account to give, that they lived in the open air, loved field-sports, and never read. And, explained in this way, Lord Beaconsfield's parallel of our aristocratic class with what he somewhat misleadingly calls the old Hellenic race appears ingenious and sound. To those lusty northerners, the Molossian or Chaonian Greeks—Greeks untouched by the development which contradistinguishes the Hellene from the barbarian—our aristocratic class, as he exhibits it, has a strong resemblance. At any rate, this class—which from its great possessions, its beauty and attractiveness, the admiration felt for it by the Philistines or middle-class, its actual

* Benjamin Disraeli (1804–81), British Prime Minister, who became Earl of Beaconsfield in 1876.—*Ed.*

power in the nation, and the still more considerable destinies to which its politeness, in Mr. Carlyle's opinion, entitles it, cannot but attract our notice pre-eminently—shows at present a great and genuine disregard for letters.

And perhaps, if there is any other body of men which strikes one, even after looking at our aristocratic class, as being in the sunshine, as exercising great attraction, as being admired by the Philistines or middle-class, and as having before it a future still more brilliant than its present, it is the friends of physical science. Now, their revolt against the tyranny of letters is notorious. To deprive letters of the too great place they have hitherto filled in men's estimation, and to substitute other studies for these, is the object of a sort of crusade with a body of people important in itself, but still more important because of the gifted leaders who march at its head.

Religion has always hitherto been a great power in England; and on this account, perhaps, whatever humiliations may be in store for religion in the future, the friends of physical science will not object to our saying, that, after them and the aristocracy, the leaders of the religious world fill a prominent place in the public eye even now, and one cannot help noticing what their opinions and likings are. And it is curious how the feeling of the chief people in the religious world, too, seems to be just now against letters, which they slight as the vague and inexact instrument of shallow essayists and magazine-writers; and in favour of dogma, of a scientific and exact presentment of religious things, instead of a literary presentment of them. "Dogmatic theology," says the *Guardian*, speaking of our existing dogmatic theology—"Dogmatic theology, *that is, precision and definiteness* of religious thought." "Maudlin sentimentalism," says the Dean of Norwich, "with its miserable disparagements of any *definite* doctrine; a *nerveless* religion, without the *sinew* and *bone* of doctrine." The distinguished Chancellor of the University of Oxford thought it needful to tell us on a public occasion lately, that "religion is no

more to be severed from *dogma* than light from the sun."
Everyone, again, remembers the Bishops of Winchester*
and Gloucester making in Convocation their remarkable
effort "to do something," as they said, "for the honour of
Our Lord's Godhead," and to mark their sense of "that infinite separation for time and for eternity which is involved
in rejecting the Godhead of the Eternal Son." In the same
way: "To no teaching," says one champion of dogma, "can
the appellation of Christian be truly given which does not
involve the idea of a Personal God." Another lays like stress
on correct ideas about the Personality of the Holy Ghost.
"Our Lord unquestionably," says a third, "annexes eternal
life to a right knowledge of the Godhead"—that is, to a
right speculative, dogmatic knowledge of it. A fourth ap-
peals to history and human nature for proof that "an un-
dogmatic Church can no more satisfy the hunger of the soul,
than a snowball, painted to look like fruit, would stay the
hunger of the stomach." And all these friends of theological
science are, like the friends of physical science, though from
another cause, severe upon letters. Attempts made at a literary treatment of religious history and ideas they call "a
subverting of the faith once delivered to the saints." Those
who make them they speak of as "those who have made
shipwreck of the faith;" and when they talk of "the poison
openly disseminated by infidels," and describe the "progress
of infidelity," which more and more, according to their account, "denies God, rejects Christ, and lets loose every
human passion," though they have the audaciousness of
physical science most in their eye, yet they have a direct
aim, too, at the looseness and dangerous temerity of letters.

Keeping in remembrance what Scripture says about the
young man who had great possessions, to be able to work a
change of mind in our aristocratic class we never have pretended, we never shall pretend. But to the friends of phys-

* Samuel Wilberforce, who was embroiled in the controversies
over biblical criticism and Darwinism.—*Ed.*

ical science and to the friends of dogma we do feel embold-
ened, after giving our best consideration to the matter, to
say a few words on behalf of letters, and in deprecation of
the slight which, on different grounds, they both put upon
them. But particularly in reply to the friends of dogma do
we wish to insist on the case for letters, because of the great
issues which seem to us to be here involved. Therefore of the
relation of letters to religion we are going now to speak; of
their effect upon dogma, and of the consequences of this to
religion. And so the subject of the present volume will be
literature and dogma.

2

Abstruse reasoning not essential to religion

It is clear that dogmatists love religion—for else why
do they occupy themselves with it so much, and make it,
most of them, the business, even the professional business, of
their lives? And clearly religion seeks man's salvation. How
distressing, therefore, must it be to them, to think that "salvation is unquestionably annexed to a right knowledge of
the Godhead," and that a right knowledge of the Godhead
depends upon reasoning, for which so many people have not
much aptitude; and upon reasoning from ideas or terms
such as substance, identity, causation, design, about which
there is endless disagreement! It is true, a right knowledge
of geometry also depends upon reasoning, and many people
never get it; but then, in the first place, salvation is not
annexed to a right knowledge of geometry; and in the
second, the ideas or terms such as *point, line, angle,* from
which we reason in geometry, are terms about which there is
no ambiguity or disagreement. But as to the demonstrations
and terms of theology we cannot comfort ourselves in this
manner. . . . And what a consolation to us, who are so perpetually being taunted with our known inaptitude for abstruse reasoning if we can find that for this great concern of

religion, at any rate, abstruse reasoning does not seem to be the appointed help; and that as good or better a help—for indeed there can hardly, to judge by the present state of things, be a worse—may be something which is in an ordinary man's power!

For the good of letters is, that they require no extraordinary acuteness such as is required to handle the theory of causation like the Archbishop of York, or the doctrine of the Godhead of the Eternal Son like the Bishops of Winchester and Gloucester. The good of letters may be had without skill in arguing, or that formidable logical apparatus, not unlike a guillotine, which Professor Huxley speaks of somewhere as the young man's best companion—and so it *would* be his best companion; no doubt, if all wisdom were come at by hard reasoning. In that case, all who could not manage this apparatus (and only a few picked craftsmen can manage it) would be in a pitiable condition.

But the valuable thing in letters—that is, in the acquainting oneself with the best which has been thought and said in the world—is, as we have often remarked, the judgment which forms itself insensibly in a fair mind along with fresh knowledge; and this judgment almost anyone with a fair mind, who will but trouble himself to try and make acquaintance with the best which has been thought and uttered in the world, may, if he is lucky, hope to attain to. For this judgment comes almost of itself; and what it displaces it displaces easily and naturally, and without any turmoil of controversial reasonings. The thing comes to look differently to us, as we look at it by the light of fresh knowledge. We are not beaten from our old opinion by logic, we are not driven off our ground—our ground itself changes with us.

Far more of our mistakes come from want of fresh knowledge than from want of correct reasoning; and, therefore, letters meet a greater want in us than does logic. The idea of a triangle is a definite and ascertained thing, and to de-

duce the properties of a triangle from it is an affair of reasoning. There are heads unapt for this sort of work, and
some of the blundering to be found in the world is from this
cause. But how far more of the blundering to be found in
the world comes from people fancying that some idea is a
definite and ascertained thing, like the idea of a triangle,
when it is not; and proceeding to deduce properties from it,
and to do battle about them, when their first start was a
mistake! And how liable are people with a talent for hard,
abstruse reasoning, to be tempted to this mistake! And what
can clear up such a mistake except a wide and familiar
acquaintance with the human spirit and its productions,
showing how ideas and terms arose, and what is their character? and this is letters and history, not logic.

So that minds with small aptitude for abstruse reasoning may yet, through letters, gain some hold on sound
judgment and useful knowledge, and may even clear up
blunders committed, out of their very excess of talent, by
the athletes of logic.

Chapter I

Religion Given

1

I have said elsewhere[1] how much it has contributed to the misunderstanding of St. Paul, that terms like *grace, new birth, justification*—which he used in a fluid and passing way, as men use terms in common discourse or in eloquence and poetry, to describe approximately, but only approximately, what they have present before their mind, but do not profess that their mind does or can grasp exactly or adequately—that such terms people have blunderingly taken in a fixed and rigid manner, as if they were symbols with as definite and fully grasped a meaning as the names *line* or *angle,* and proceeded to use them on this supposition. Terms, in short, which with St. Paul are *literary* terms, theologians have employed as if they were *scientific* terms.

Ambiguity connected with the term of God

But if one desires to deal with this mistake thoroughly, one must observe it in that supreme term with which religion is filled—the term *God.* The seemingly incurable ambiguity in the mode of employing this word is at the root of all our religious differences and difficulties. People use it as if it stood for a perfectly definite and ascertained idea, from which we might, without more ado, extract propositions and draw inferences, just as we should from any other definite and ascertained idea. For instance, I open a book which controverts what its author thinks dangerous views about religion, and I read: "Our sense of morality tells us so-

[1] *Culture and Anarchy.*

and-so." And again, 'the impulse in man to seek God," is distinguished, as if the distinction were self-evident and explained itself, from "the impulse in man to seek his highest perfection." Now, *morality* represents for everybody a thoroughly definite and ascertained idea—the idea of human conduct regulated in a certain manner. Everybody, again, understands distinctly enough what is meant by man's perfection—his reaching the best which his powers and circumstances allow him to reach. And the word "God" is used, in connexion with both these words, morality and perfection, as if it stood for just as definite and ascertained an idea as they do; an idea drawn from experience, just as the ideas are which they stand for; an idea about which everyone was agreed, and from which we might proceed to argue and to make inferences, with certainty that, as in the case of morality and perfection, the basis on which we were going everyone knew and granted. But, in truth, the word "God" is used in most cases as by no means a term of science or exact knowledge, but a term of poetry and eloquence, a term *thrown out*, so to speak, at a not fully grasped object of the speaker's consciousness, a *literary* term, in short; and mankind mean different things by it as their consciousness differs.

The first question, then is how people are using the word; whether in this literary way, or in a scientific way. The second question is, what, supposing them to use the term as one of poetry and eloquence, and to import into it, therefore, a great deal of their own individual feelings and character, is yet the common substratum of idea on which in using it, they all rest. For this will then be, for them, and for us in dealing with them, the real sense of the word; the sense in which we can use it for purposes of argument and inference without ambiguity.

Strictly and formally the word "God," so some philologists tell us, means, like its kindred Aryan words, *Theos, Deus,* and *Deva,* simply *shining* or *brilliant.* In a certain narrow way, therefore, this would be (if the etymology is right) the one exact and scientific sense of the word. It was long thought, however, to mean *good,* and so Luther took it to mean *the best that man knows or can know;* and in this sense, as a matter of fact and history, mankind constantly use the word. This is the common substratum of idea on which men in general, when they use the word *God,* rest; and we can take this as the word's real sense fairly enough, only it does not give us anything very precise.

But then there is also the scientific sense held by theologians, deduced from the ideas of substance, identity, causation, design, and so on; but taught, they say, or at least implied, in the Bible, and on which all the Bible rests. According to this scientific and theological sense—which has all the outward appearances, at any rate, of great precision —God is an infinite and eternal substance, and at the same time a person, the great first cause, the moral and intelligent governor of the universe; Jesus Christ consubstantial with him; and the Holy Ghost a person proceeding from the other two. This is the sense for which, or for portions of which, the Bishops of Winchester and Gloucester are so zealous to do something.

Other people, however, who fail to perceive the force of such a deduction from the abstract ideas above mentioned, who indeed think it quite hollow, but who are told that this sense is in the Bible, and that they must receive it if they receive the Bible, conclude that in that case they had better receive neither the one nor the other. Something of this sort it was no doubt, which made Professor Huxley tell the London School Board lately, that "if these islands had no religion at all, it would not enter into his mind to introduce the religious idea by the agency of the Bible." Of such people there are now a great many; and indeed there could hardly, for those who value the Bible, be a greater example of the sacrifices one is sometimes called upon to make for the truth, than to find that for the truth as held by the Bishops of Winchester and Gloucester, if it is the truth, one must sacrifice the allegiance of so many people to the Bible.

Religion has to do with conduct

But surely, if there be anything with which metaphysics have nothing to do, and where a plain man, without skill to walk in the arduous paths of abstruse reasoning, may yet find himself at home, it is religion. For the object of religion is *conduct*; and conduct is really, however men may overlay it with philosophical disquisitions, the simplest thing in the world. That is to say, it is the simplest thing in the world as far as *understanding* is concerned; as regards *doing*, it is the hardest thing in the world. Here is the difficulty—to *do* what we very well know ought to be done; and instead of facing this, men have searched out another with which they occupy themselves by preference—the origin of what is called the moral sense, the genesis and physiology of con-science, and so on. No one denies that here, too, is difficulty, or that the difficulty is a proper object for the human facul-ties to be exercised upon; but the difficulty here is specula-tive. It is not the difficulty of religion, which is a practical one; and it often tends to divert the attention from this. Yet surely the difficulty of religion is great enough by itself, if men would but consider it, to satisfy the most voracious ap-petite for difficulties. It extends to rightness in the whole range of what we call *conduct*; in three-fourths, therefore, at the very lowest computation, of human life. The only doubt is whether we ought not to make the range of conduct wider still, and to say it is four-fifths of human life, or five-sixths. But it is better to be under the mark than over it; so let us be content with reckoning conduct as three-fourths of hu-man life.

And to recognise in what way conduct is this, let us eschew all school-terms, like *moral sense*, and *volitional*, and *altruistic*, which philosophers employ, and let us help our-selves by the most palpable and plain examples. When the rich man in the Bible-parable says: "Soul, thou hast much goods laid up for many years; take thine ease, eat, drink,

and be merry!" [2]—those *goods* which he thus assigns as the
stuff with which human life is mainly concerned (and so in
practice it really is) —those goods and our dealings with
them—our taking our ease, eating, drinking, being merry,
are the matter of *conduct*, the range where it is exercised.
Eating, drinking, ease, pleasure, money, the intercourse of
the sexes, the giving free swing to one's temper and instincts
—these are the matters with which conduct is concerned,
and with which all mankind know and feel it to be concerned. . . . But it is evident, if conduct deals with these,
both how important a thing conduct is, and how simple a
thing. Important, because it covers so large a portion of
human life, and the portion common to all sorts of people;
simple, because, though there needs perpetual admonition to
form conduct, the admonition is needed not to determine
what we ought to do, but to make us do it.

And as to this simplicity, all moralists are agreed. "Let
any plain honest man," says Bishop Butler, "before he en-
gages in any course of action" (he means action of the very
kind we call *conduct*) , "ask himself: Is this I am going
about right or is it wrong? is it good or is it evil? I do not in
the least doubt but that this question would be answered
agreeably to truth and virtue by *almost any fair man in
almost any circumstance.*" And Bishop Wilson says: "Look
up to God" (by which he means just this: Consult your
conscience) "at all times, and he will, *as in a glass*, discover
what is fit to be done." And the Preacher's well-known sentence is exactly to the same effect: "God *made man upright*;
but they have sought out many inventions," [3]—or, as it
more correctly is, *"many abstruse reasonings."* Let us hold
fast to this, and we shall find we have a stay by the help of
which even poor weak men, with no pretensions to be logical athletes, may stand firmly.

And so, when we are asked, what is the object of re-

[2] Luke 12:19.   [3] Ecclesiastes 7:29.

ligion?—let us reply: *Conduct.* And when we are asked further, what is conduct?—let us answer: *Three-fourths of life.*

2

And certainly we need not go far about to prove that conduct, or "righteousness," which is the object of religion, is in a special manner the object of Bible-religion. The word "righteousness" is the master-word of the Old Testament. *Keep judgment and do righteousness! Cease to do evil, learn to do well!* [4] these words being taken in their plainest sense of conduct. *Offer the sacrifice,* not of victims and ceremonies, as the way of the world in religion then was, but: Offer the sacrifice of *righteousness!* [5] The great concern of the New Testament is likewise righteousness, but righteousness reached through particular means, righteousness by the means of Jesus Christ. A sentence which sums up the New Testament and assigns the ground whereon the Christian Church stands, is, as we have elsewhere said, [6] this: *Let every one that nameth the name of Christ depart from iniquity!* [7] If we are to take a sentence which in like manner sums up the Old Testament, such a sentence is this: *O ye that love the Eternal, see that ye hate the thing which is evil! to him that ordereth his conversation right shall be shown the salvation of God.* [8]

But instantly there will be raised the objection that this is morality, not religion; morality, ethics, conduct, being by many people, and above all by theologians, carefully contradistinguished from religion, which is supposed in some special way to be connected with propositions about the Godhead of the Eternal Son, or propositions about the personality of God, or about election or justification. Religion,

---

[4] Isaiah 56:1; 1:16–17.
[5] Psalms 4:5.
[6] *St. Paul and Protestantism.*
[7] II Timothy 2:19.
[8] Psalms 97:10; 50:23.

however, means simply either a binding to righteousness, or else a serious attending to righteousness and dwelling upon it. Which of these two it most nearly means, depends upon the view we take of the word's derivation; but it means one of them, and they are really much the same. And the antithesis between *ethical* and *religious* is thus quite a false one. Ethical means *practical*, it relates to practice or conduct passing into habit or disposition. Religious also means *practical*, but practical in a still higher degree; and the right antithesis to both ethical and religious, is the same as the right antithesis to practical: namely, *theoretical*.

Religion is morality touched by emotion

Now, propositions about the Godhead of the Eternal Son are theoretical, and they therefore are very properly opposed to propositions which are moral or ethical; but they are with equal propriety opposed to propositions which are religious. They differ in kind from what is religious, while what is ethical agrees in kind with it. But is there, therefore, no difference between what is ethical, or morality, and religion? There *is* a difference; a difference of degree. Religion, if we follow the intention of human thought and human language in the use of the word, is ethics heightened, enkindled, lit up by feeling; the passage from morality to religion is made when to morality is applied emotion. And the true meaning of religion is thus, not simply *morality*, but *morality touched by emotion*. And this new elevation and inspiration of morality is well marked by the word "righteousness." Conduct is the word of common life, morality is the word of philosophical disquisition, righteousness is the word of religion.

Some people, indeed, are for calling all high thought and feeling by the name of religion; according to that saying of Goethe: "He who has art and science, has also religion." But let us use words as mankind generally use them. We may call art and science touched by emotion *religion*, if we will; as we may make the instinct of self-preservation, into which M. Littré traces up all our private affections, include the perfecting ourselves by the study of what is beautiful in art; and the reproductive instinct, into which he traces up all our social affections, include the perfecting mankind by political science. But men have not yet got to that stage, when we think much of either their private or their social affections at all, except as exercising themselves in conduct; neither do we yet think of religion as otherwise exercising itself. When mankind speak of religion, they have before their mind an activity engaged, not with the whole of life, but with that three-fourths of life which is *conduct*. This is wide enough range for one word, surely; but at any rate, let us at present limit ourselves in the use of the word *religion* as mankind do.

And if some one now asks: But what *is* this application of emotion to morality, and by what marks may we know it?—we can quite easily satisfy him; not, indeed, by any disquisition of our own, but in a much better way, by examples. "By the dispensation of Providence to mankind," says Quintilian, "goodness gives men most satisfaction." That is morality. "The path of the just is as the shining light which shineth more and more unto the perfect day." That is morality touched with emotion, or religion. "Hold off from sensuality," says Cicero; "for, if you have given yourself up to it, you will find yourself unable to think of anything else." That is morality. "Blessed are the pure in heart," says Jesus Christ; "for they shall see God." That is religion. "We all want to live honestly, but cannot," says the Greek maxim-maker. That is morality. "O wretched man that I am, who shall deliver me from the body of this death!" says St. Paul.[9] That is religion. "Would thou wert of as good conversation in deed as in word!" is morality. "Not every one that saith unto me, Lord, Lord, shall enter into the Kingdom of Heaven, but he that doeth the will of

[9] Romans 7:24.

my Father which is in Heaven," [10] is religion. "Live as you were meant to live!" is morality. "Lay hold on eternal life!" [11] is religion.

Or we may take the contrast within the bounds of the Bible itself. "Love not sleep, lest thou come to poverty," is morality. But: "My meat is to do the will of him that sent me, and to finish his work," is religion.[12] Or we may even observe a third stage between these two stages, which shows to us the transition from one to the other. "If thou givest thy soul the desire that please her, she will make thee a laughing stock to thine enemies" [13]—that is morality. "He that resisteth pleasures crowneth his life" [14]—that is morality with the tone heightened, passing, or trying to pass, into religion. "Flesh and blood cannot inherit the kingdom of God" [15]—there the passage is made, and we have religion. Our religious examples are here all taken from the Bible, and from the Bible such examples can best be taken; but we might also find them elsewhere. "Oh that my lot might lead me in the path of holy innocence of thought and deed, the path which august laws ordain, laws which in the highest heaven had their birth, neither did the race of mortal man beget them, nor shall oblivion ever put them to sleep; the power of God is mighty in them, and groweth not old!" That is from Sophocles, but it is as much religion as any of the things which we have quoted as religious. Like them, it is not the mere enjoining of conduct, but it is this enjoining touched, strengthened, and almost transformed, by the addition of feeling.

So what is meant by the application of emotion to morality has now, it is to be hoped, been made clear. The next question will probably be: but how does one get the application made? Why, how does one get to feel much about any matter whatever? By dwelling upon it, by staying

[10] Matthew 7:21.
[11] I Timothy 6:12.
[12] Proverbs 20:13; John 4:34.
[13] Ecclesiasticus 18:31.
[14] Ecclesiasticus 19:5.
[15] I Corinthians 20:50.

our thoughts upon it, by having it perpetually in our mind. The very words *mind, memory, remain,* come, probably, all from the same root, from the notion of staying, attending. Possibly even the word *man* comes from the same; so entirely does the idea of humanity, of intelligence, of looking before and after, of raising oneself out of the flux of things, rest upon the idea of steadying oneself, concentrating oneself, making order in the chaos of one's impressions, by attending to one impression rather than the other. The rules of conduct, of morality, were themselves, philosophers suppose, reached in this way—the notion of a whole self as opposed to a partial self, a best self to an inferior self, to a momentary self a permanent self requiring the restraint of impulses a man would naturally have indulged; because, by *attending* to his life, man found it had a scope beyond the wants of the present moment. Suppose it was so; then the first man who, as "a being," comparatively, "of a large discourse, looking before and after," controlled the native, instantaneous, mechanical impulses of the instinct of self-preservation, controlled the native, instantaneous, mechanical impulses of the reproductive instinct, had morality revealed to him.

But there is a long way from this to that habitual dwelling on the rules thus reached, that constant turning them over in the mind, that near and lively experimental sense of their beneficence, which communicates emotion to our thought of them, and thus incalculably heightens their power. And the more mankind attended to the claims of that part of our nature which does *not* belong to conduct, properly so called, or to morality (and we have seen that, after all, about one-fourth of our nature is in this case), the more they would have distractions to take off their thoughts from those moral conclusions which all races of men, one may say, seem to have reached, and to prevent these moral conclusions from being quickened by emotion, and thus becoming religious.

3

Only with one people—the people from whom we get
the Bible—these distractions did not so much happen.

The Old Testament, nobody will ever deny, is filled
with the word and thought of righteousness. "In the way of
righteousness is life, and in the pathway thereof is no
death"; "Righteousness tendeth to life"; "He that pursueth
evil pursueth it to his own death"; "The way of transgres-
sors is hard"—nobody will deny that those texts may stand
for the fundamental and ever-recurring idea of the Old
Testament.[16] No people ever felt so strongly as the people
of the Old Testament, the Hebrew people, that conduct is
three-fourths of our life and its largest concern. No people
ever felt so strongly that succeeding, going right, hitting the
mark in this great concern, was *the way of peace*, the highest
possible satisfaction. "He that keepeth the law, happy is he;
its ways are ways of pleasantness, and all its paths are peace;
if thou hadst walked in its ways, thou shouldst have dwelt in
peace for ever!" [17] Jeshurun, one of the ideal names of their
race, is the *upright*; Israel, the other and greater, is the
wrestler with God, he who has known the contention and
strain it costs to stand upright. That mysterious personage
by whom their history first touches the hill of Sion, is
Melchisedek, the *righteous* king. Their holy city, Jerusalem,
is the foundation, or vision, or inheritance, of that which
righteousness achieves—*peace*. The law of righteousness was
such an object of attention to them, that its words were to
"be in their heart, and thou shalt teach them diligently
unto thy children, and shalt talk of them when thou sittest
in thine house, and when thou walkest by the way, and
when thou liest down, and when thou risest up." [18] That

---

[16] Proverbs 12:28; 11:19; 13:15.
[17] Proverbs 29:18; 3:17; Baruch 3:13.
[18] Deuteronomy 6:6–7.

they might keep them ever in mind, they wore them, went about with them, made talismans of them: "Bind them upon thy fingers, bind them about thy neck; write them upon the table of thine heart!" [19] "Take fast hold of her," they said of the doctrine of conduct, or righteousness, "let her not go! keep her, for *she is thy life!*" [20]

The part in righteousness not ourselves

People who thus spoke of righteousness could not but have had their minds long and deeply engaged with it; much more than the generality of mankind, who `have nevertheless, as we saw, got as far as the notion of morals or conduct. And, if they were so deeply attentive to it, one thing could not fail to strike them. It is this: the very great part in righteousness which belongs, we may say, to *not ourselves.* In the first place, we did not make ourselves and our nature, or conduct as the object of three-fourths of that nature; we did not provide that happiness should follow conduct, as it undeniably does; that the sense of succeeding, going right, hitting the mark, in conduct, should give satisfaction, and a very high satisfaction, just as really as the sense of doing well in his work gives pleasure to a man who is learning to ride or to shoot; or as satisfying his hunger, also, gives pleasure to a man who is hungry.

All this we did not make; and, in the next place, our dealing with it at all, when it is made, is not wholly, or even nearly wholly, in our own power. Our conduct is capable, irrespective of what we can ourselves certainly answer for, of almost infinitely different degrees of force and energy in the performance of it, of lucidity and vividness in the perception of it, of fulness in the satisfaction from it; and these degrees may vary from day to day, and quite incalculably. Facilities and felicities—whence do they come? suggestions and stimulations—where do they tend? hardly a day passes but we have some experience of them. And so Henry More

[19] Proverbs 7:3; 3:3.   [20] Proverbs 4:13.

was led to say, that "there was something about us that knew better, often, what we would be at than we ourselves." For instance: everyone can understand how health and freedom from pain may give energy for conduct, and how a neuralgia, suppose, may diminish it. It does not depend on ourselves, indeed, whether we have the neuralgia or not, but we can understand its impairing our spirit. But the strange thing is, that with the same neuralgia we may find ourselves one day without spirit and energy for conduct, and another day with them. So that we may most truly say, with the author of the *Imitation*: "Left to ourselves, we sink and perish; visited, we lift up our heads and live." And we may well give ourselves, in grateful and devout self-surrender, to that by which we are thus visited. So much is there incalculable, so much that belongs to *not ourselves*, in conduct; and the more we attend to conduct, and the more we value it, the more we shall feel this.

The *not ourselves*, which is in us and the world around us, has almost everywhere, as far as we can see, struck the minds of men as they awoke to consciousness, and has inspired them with awe. Everyone knows how the mighty natural objects which most took their regards became the objects to which this awe addressed itself. Our very word *God* is, perhaps, a reminiscence of these times, when men invoked "The Brilliant on high," *sublime hoc candens quod invocant omnes Jovem,* as the power representing to them that which transcended the limits of their narrow selves, and by which they lived and moved and had their being. Everyone knows of what differences of operation men's dealing with this power has in different places and times shown itself capable; how here they have been moved by the *not ourselves* to a cruel terror, there to a timid religiosity, there again to a play of imagination; almost always, however, connecting with it, by some string or other, conduct.

But we are not writing a history of religion; we are only tracing its effect on the language of the men from whom we get the Bible. At the time they produced those documents which give to the Old Testament its power and its true character, the *not ourselves* which weighed upon the mind of Israel, and engaged its awe, was the *not ourselves* by which we get the sense for *righteousness*, and whence we find the help to *do right*. This conception was indubitably what lay at the bottom of that remarkable change which under Moses, at a certain stage of their religious history, befell the Hebrew people's mode of naming God.[21] This was what they intended in that name, which we wrongly convey, either without translation, by *Jehovah,* which gives us the notion of a mere mythological deity, or by a wrong translation, *Lord,* which gives us the notion of a magnified and non-natural man. The name they used was: *The Eternal.*

The Eternal not ourselves
comes from moral experience
not metaphysical speculation

Philosophers dispute whether moral ideas, as they call them, the simplest ideas of conduct and righteousness which now seem instinctive, did not all grow, were not once inchoate, embryo, dubious, unformed. That may have been so; the question is an interesting one for science. But the interesting question for conduct is whether those ideas are unformed or formed *now*. They are formed now; and they were formed when the Hebrews named the power, not of their own making, which pressed upon their spirit: *The Eternal.* Probably the life of Abraham, *the friend of God,* however imperfectly the Bible traditions by themselves convey it to us, was a decisive step forwards in the development of these ideas of righteousness. Probably this was the moment when such ideas became fixed and ruling for the Hebrew people, and marked it permanently off from all other peoples who had not made the same step. But long

[21] Exodus 3:14.

before the first beginnings of recorded history, long before the oldest word of Bible literature, these ideas must have been at work. We know it by the result, although they may have for a long while been but rudimentary. In Israel's earliest history and earliest utterances, under the name of Eloah, Elohim, *The Mighty*, there may have lain and matured, there did lie and mature, ideas of God more as a moral power, more as a power connected, above everything, with conduct and righteousness, than were entertained by other races. Not only can we judge the result that this must have been so, but we can see that it was so. Still their name, *The Mighty*, does not in itself involve any true and deep religious ideas, any more than our Aryan name, *Deva, Deus, The Shining*. With *The Eternal* it is otherwise. For what did they mean by the Eternal; the Eternal *what*? The Eternal *cause*? Alas, these poor people were not Archbishops of York. They meant the Eternal *righteous*, who loveth *righteousness*. They had dwelt upon the thought of conduct, and of right and wrong, until the *not ourselves*, which is in us and all around us, became to them adorable eminently and altogether *as a power which makes for righteousness*; which makes for it unchangeably and eternally, and is therefore called *The Eternal*.

There is not a particle of metaphysics in their use of this name, any more than in their conception of the *not ourselves* to which they attached it. Both came to them not from abstruse reasoning but from experience, and from experience in the plain region of conduct. Theologians with metaphysical heads render Israel's *Eternal* by *the self-existent*, and Israel's *not ourselves* by *the absolute*, and attribute to Israel their own subtleties. According to them, Israel had his head full of the necessity of a first cause, and therefore, said, *The Eternal*; as, again, they imagine him looking out into the world, noting everywhere the marks of design and adaptation to his wants, and reasoning out and inferring thence the fatherhood of God. All these fancies come from an excessive turn for reasoning, and from a neglect of observing men's actual course of thinking and way of using words. Israel, at this stage when *The Eternal* was revealed to him, inferred nothing, reasoned out nothing; he felt and experienced. When he begins to speculate, in the schools of Rabbinism, he quickly shows how much less native talent than the Bishops of Winchester and Gloucester he has for this perilous business. Happily, when *The Eternal* was revealed to him, he had not yet begun to speculate.

Israel personified, indeed, his Eternal, for he was strongly moved, he was an orator and poet. *Man never knows how anthropomorphic he is,* says Goethe; and so man tends always to represent everything under his own figure. In poetry and eloquence man may and must follow this tendency, but in science it often leads him astray. Israel, however, did not scientifically predicate *personality* of God; he would not even have had a notion what was meant by it. He called him the maker of all things, who gives drink to all out of his pleasures as out of a river; but he was led to this by no theory of a first cause. The grandeur of the spectacle given by the world, the grandeur of the sense of its all being *not ourselves,* being above and beyond ourselves and immeasurably dwarfing us, a man of imagination instinctively personifies as a single, mighty, living and productive power; as Goethe tells us that the words which rose naturally to his lips, when he stood on the top of the Brocken, were: "Lord, what is man, that thou mindest him, or the son of man, that thou makest account of him?" [22] But Israel's confessing and extolling of this power came not even from his imaginative feeling, but came first from his gratitude for righteousness. To one who knows what conduct is, it is a joy to be alive; and the *not ourselves,* which by bringing forth for us righteousness makes our happiness, working just in the same sense, brings forth this glorious world to be righteous in. That is the notion at the bottom of the Hebrew's praise of a Creator; and if we attend, we can see this quite clearly.

[22] Psalms 144:3.

Wisdom and understanding mean, for Israel, the love of order, of righteousness. Righteousness, order, conduct, is for Israel at once the source of all man's happiness, and at the same time the very essence of *The Eternal*. The great work of the Eternal is the foundation of this order in man, the implanting in mankind of his own love of righteousness, his own spirit, his own wisdom and understanding; and it is only as a farther and natural working of this energy that Israel conceives the establishment of order in the world, or creation. "To depart from evil, *that* is understanding! Happy is the man that findeth wisdom, and the man that getteth understanding! *The Eternal by wisdom hath founded the earth, by understanding hath he established the heavens*"; [23] and so the Bible-writer passes into the account of creation. It all comes to him from the idea of righteousness.

And it is the same with all the language our Hebrew religionist uses. God is a father, because the power in and around us, which makes for righteousness, is indeed best described by the name of this authoritative but yet tender and protecting relation. So, too, with the intense fear and abhorrence of idolatry. Conduct, righteousness, is, above all, a matter of inward motion and rule. No sensible forms can represent it, or help us to it; such attempts at representation can only distract us from it. So, too, with the sense of the oneness of God. "Hear, O Israel! The Lord our God is one Lord." [24] People think that in this unity of God—this monotheistic idea, as they call it—they have certainly got metaphysics at last. They have got nothing of the kind. The monotheistic idea of Israel is simply *seriousness*. There are, indeed, many aspects of the *not ourselves*; but Israel regarded one aspect of it only, that by which it makes for righteousness. . . .

[23] Job 28:28; Proverbs 3:13, 19.
[24] Deuteronomy 6:4.

Language of the Bible literary, not scientific

And in spite of his turn for personification, his want of
a clear boundary-line between poetry and science, his inaptitude to express even abstract notions by other than highly
concrete terms—in spite of these scientific disadvantages, or
rather, perhaps, because of them, because he had no talent
for abstruse reasoning to lead him astray—the spirit and
tongue of Israel kept a propriety, a reserve, a sense of the
inadequacy of language in conveying man's ideas of God,
which contrast strongly with the licence of affirmation in
our Western theology. "The high and lofty One that in-
habiteth eternity, whose name is holy," [25] is far more
proper and felicitous language than "the moral and intelligent Governor of the universe," just because it far less attempts to be precise, but keeps to the language of poetry
and does not essay the language of science. As he had
developed his idea of God from personal experience, Israel
knew what we, who have developed our idea from his words
about it, so often are ignorant of: that his words were but
thrown out at a vast object of consciousness, which he could
not fully grasp, and which he apprehended clearly by one
point alone—that it made for the great concern of life, *conduct.* . . .

4

The language of the Bible, then, is literary, not scientific language; language *thrown out* at an object of consciousness not fully grasped, which inspired emotion. Evidently, if the object be one not fully to be grasped, and one
to inspire emotion, the language of figure and feeling will
satisfy us better about it, will cover more of what we seek to
express, than the language of literal fact and science. The

25 Isaiah 57:15.

language of science about it will be *below* what we feel to be the truth.

An attempt at defining the term God

The question however has risen and confronts us: what *was* the scientific basis of fact for this consciousness? When we have once satisfied ourselves both as to the tentative, poetic way in which the Bible authors used language, and also as to their having no pretensions to metaphysics at all, let us, therefore, when there is this question raised as to the scientific account of what they had before their minds, be content with a very unpretending answer. And in this way such a phrase as that which I have formerly used concerning God, and have been much blamed for using—the phrase, namely, that, "for science, God is simply *the stream of tendency by which all things seek to fulfil the law of their being* —may be allowed, and may even prove useful. Certainly it is inadequate; certainly it is a less proper phrase than, for instance: "Clouds and darkness are round about him, righteousness and judgment are the habitation of his seat." [26] But then it is, in however humble a degree and with however narrow a reach, a *scientific* definition, which the other is not. The phrase, "A Personal First Cause, the moral and intelligent Governor of the universe," has also, when applied to God, the character, no doubt, of a scientific definition. But then it goes far beyond what is admittedly certain and verifiable, which is what we mean by scientific. It attempts far too much. If we want here, as we do want, to have what is admittedly certain and verifiable, we must con-

---

[26] Psalms 97:2. It has been urged that if the personifying mode of expression is more proper, it must, also, be more scientifically exact. But surely it will on reflexion appear that this is by no means so. Wordsworth calls the earth "the mighty mother of mankind," and the geographers call her "an oblate spheroid"; Wordsworth's expression is more proper and adequate to convey what men feel about the earth, but it is not therefore the more scientifically exact.

tent ourselves with very little. No one will say, that it is admittedly certain and verifiable, that there is a personal first cause, the moral and intelligent governor of the universe, whom we may call *God* if we will. But that all things seem to us to have what we call a law of their being, and to tend to fulfil it, is certain and admitted; though whether we will call this *God* or not, is a matter of choice. Suppose, however, we call it *God*, we then give the name of *God* to a certain and admitted reality; this, at least is an advantage.

And the notion of our definition does, in fact, enter into the term *God*, in men's common use of it. To please God, to serve God, to obey God's will, means to follow a law of things which is found in conscience, and which is an indication, irrespective of our arbitrary wish and fancy, of what we ought to do. There *is*, then, a real power which makes for righteousness; and it is the greatest of realities for us.[27] When St. Paul says, that our business is "to serve the spirit of God," "to serve the living and true God"; [28] and when Epictetus says: "What do I want?—to acquaint myself with the natural order of things, and comply with it," they both mean, so far, the same, in that they both mean we should obey a tendency, which is *not ourselves* but which appears in our consciousness, by which things fulfil the real law of their being. . . .

The connection between conduct and happiness

To feel that one is fulfilling in any way the law of one's being, that one is succeeding and hitting the mark, brings, as we know, happiness; to feel this in regard to so great a

[27] Prayer, about which so much has often been said unadvisedly and ill, deals with this reality. All good and beneficial prayer is in truth, however men may describe it, at bottom nothing else than an energy of aspiration towards the eternal *not ourselves* that makes for righteousness,—of aspiration towards it, and of co-operation with it. Nothing, therefore, can be more efficacious, more right, and more real.

[28] Philippians 3:3; I Thessalonians 1:9.

thing as conduct, brings, of course, happiness proportionate to the thing's greatness. We have already had Quintilian's witness, how right conduct gives joy. Who could value knowledge more than Goethe? but he marks it as being without question a lesser source of joy than conduct. Conduct he ranks with health as beyond all compare primary. "Nothing, *after* health and *virtue*," he says, "can give so much satisfaction as learning and knowing." . . .

Now, there can be no sanction to compare, for force, with the strong sanction of happiness, if it be true what Bishop Butler, who is here but the mouthpiece of humanity itself, says so irresistibly: "It is manifest that nothing can be of consequence to mankind, or any creature, but happiness." But we English are taunted with our proneness to an unworthy eudaemonism, and an Anglican bishop may perhaps be a suspected witness. Let us call, then, a glorious father of the Catholic Church, the great Augustine himself. Says St. Augustine: "Act we *must* in pursuance of what gives us most delight; *quod amplius nos delectat, secundum id operemur* necesse est."

And now let us see how exactly Israel's perceptions about God follow and confirm this simple line, which we have here reached quite independently. First: "It is *joy* to the just to do judgment." [29] Then: "It becometh well the just to be thankful." [30] Finally: "A pleasant thing is to be thankful." [31] What can be simpler than this, and at the same time more solid? But again: "The statutes of the *Eternal* rejoice the heart." [32] And then: "I will give thanks unto thee, O *Eternal*, with my whole heart; at midnight will I rise to give thanks unto thee because of thy righteous judgments!" [33] And lastly: "It is a good thing to give thanks unto the *Eternal*; it is a good thing to sing praises unto our God!" [34] Why, these are the very same propositions as the

[29] Proverbs 21:15.
[30] Psalms 33:1.
[31] Psalms 147:1.
[32] Psalms 19:8.
[33] Psalms 138:1; 119:62.
[34] Psalms 92:1; 147:1.

preceding, only with a power and depth of emotion added! Emotion has been applied to morality.

The moral use of religious language

God or *Eternal* is here really, at bottom, nothing but a deeply moved way of saying "the power that makes for *conduct* or *righteousness*." "Trust in *God*" is, in a deeply moved way of expression, the trust in the law of conduct; "delight in *the Eternal*" is, in a deeply moved way of expression, the happiness we all feel to spring from conduct. Attending to conduct, to judgment, makes the attender feel that it is joy to do it. Attending to it more still, makes him feel that it is the commandment of the Eternal, and that the joy got from it is joy got from fulfilling the commandment of the Eternal. The thankfulness for this joy is thankfulness to the Eternal; and to the Eternal, again, is due that further joy which comes from this thankfulness. "The fear of the Eternal, that is wisdom; and to depart from evil, that is understanding." [35] *"The fear of the Eternal"* and *"To depart from evil"* here mean, and are put to mean, and by the very laws of Hebrew composition which make the second phrase in a parallelism repeat the first in other words, they *must* mean, just the same thing. Yet what man of soul, after he had once risen to feel that to depart from evil was to walk in awful observance of an enduring clue, within us and without us, which leads to happiness, but would prefer to say, instead of "to depart from evil," "the fear of the Eternal"?

Henceforth, then, Israel transferred to this Eternal all his obligations. Instead of saying: "Whoso keepeth the commandment keepeth his own soul," [36] he rather said, "My soul, wait thou only upon *God*, for of him cometh my salvation!" [37] Instead of saying: "Bind them [the laws of righteousness] continually upon thine heart, and tie them

[35] Job 28:28.   [36] Proverbs 19:16.
[37] Psalms 62:5, 1.

about thy neck!" [38] he rather said, "Have I not remembered *Thee* on my bed, and thought upon *Thee* when I was waking?" [39] The obligation of a grateful and devout self-surrender to the Eternal replaced all sense of obligation to one's own better self, one's own permanent interest. The moralist's rule: "Take thought for your permanent, not your momentary, well-being," became now: "Honour *the Eternal*, not doing thine own ways, nor finding thine own pleasure, nor speaking thine own words." [40] That is, with Israel *religion* replaced *morality*.

It is true, out of the humble yet divine ground of attention to conduct, of care for what in conduct is right and good, grew morality and religion both; but, from the time when the soul felt the motive of religion, it dropped and could not but drop the other. And the motive of doing right, to a sincere soul, is now really no longer his own welfare, but *to please God*; and it bewilders his consciousness if you tell him that he does right out of *self-love*. So that, as we have said that the first man who, as "a being of a large discourse, looking before and after," controlled the blind momentary impulses of the instinct of self preservation, and controlled the blind momentary impulses of the sexual instinct, had *morality* revealed to him; so in like manner we may say, that the first man who was thrilled with gratitude, devotion, and awe, at the sense of joy and peace, not of his own making, which followed the exercise of this self-control, had *religion* revealed to him. And, for us at least, this man was Israel.

No antithesis between natural and revealed religion

Now here, as we have already pointed out the falseness of the common antithesis between *ethical* and *religious*, let us anticipate the objection that the religion here spoken of

[38] Proverbs 6:21.   [39] Psalms 63:6.
[40] Isaiah 58:13.

is but natural religion, by pointing out the falseness of the common antithesis, also, between *natural* and *revealed*. For that in us which is really natural is, in truth, *revealed*. We awake to the consciousness of it, we are aware of it coming forth in our mind; but we feel that we did not make it, that it is discovered to us, that it is what it is whether we will or no. If we are little concerned about it, we say it is *natural*; if much, we say it is *revealed*. But the difference between the two is not one of kind, only of degree. The real antithesis, to natural and revealed alike, is *invented, artificial*. Religion springing out of an experience of the power, the grandeur, the necessity of righteousness, is revealed religion, whether we find it in Sophocles or in Isaiah. "The will of mortal men did not beget it, neither shall oblivion ever put it to sleep." A system of theological notions about personality, essence, existence, consubstantiality, is *artificial* religion, and is the proper opposite to *revealed*; since it is a religion which comes forth in no one's consciousness, but is invented by theologians—able men with uncommon talents for abstruse reasoning. This religion is in no sense revealed, just because it is in no sense natural. And revealed religion is properly so named, just in proportion as it is in a pre-eminent degree natural.

The religion of the Bible, therefore, is well said to be revealed, because the great natural truth, that "righteousness tendeth to life," [41] is seized and exhibited there with such incomparable force and efficacy. All, or very nearly all, the nations of mankind have recognised the importance of conduct, and have attributed to it a natural obligation. They, however, looked at *conduct*, not as something full of happiness and joy, but as something one could not manage to do without. But: "Sion heard it and *rejoiced*, and the daughters of Judah were *glad*, because of thy judgments, O Eternal!" [42] Happiness is our being's end and aim, and no one has ever come near Israel in feeling, and in making

[41] Proverbs 11:19.   [42] Psalms 97:8.

others feel, that *to righteousness belongs happiness!* The prodigies and the marvellous of Bible-religion are common to it with all religions; the love of righteousness, in this eminency, is its own. . . .

5

Israel's witness to the world

Now manifestly this sense of [Israel's] has a double force for the rest of mankind—an evidential force and a practical force. Its evidential force is in keeping men's view, by the example of the signal apparition, in one branch of our race, of the sense for conduct and righteousness, the reality and naturalness of that sense. Clearly, unless a sense or endowment of human nature, however in itself real and beneficent, has some signal representative among mankind, it tends to be pressed upon by other senses and endowments, to suffer from its own want of energy, and to be more and more pushed out of sight. . . .

Then there is the practical force of their example; and this is even more important. Everyone is aware how those, who want to cultivate any sense or endowment in themselves, must be habitually conversant with the works of people who have been eminent for that sense, must study them, catch inspiration from them. Only in this way, indeed, can progress be made. And as long as the world lasts, all who want to make progress in righteousness will come to Israel for inspiration, as to the people who have had the sense for righteousness most glowing and strongest; and in hearing and reading the words Israel has uttered for us, carers for conduct will find a glow and a force they could find nowhere else. . . .

This does truly constitute for Israel a most extraordinary distinction. In spite of all which in them and in their character is unattractive, nay, repellent—in spite of their shortcomings even in righteousness itself and their insignificance in everything else—this petty, unsuccessful, unamiable people, without politics, without science, without art, without charm, deserve their great place in the world's regard, and are likely to have it more, as the world goes on, rather than less. It is secured to them by the facts of human nature, and by the unalterable constitution of things. "God hath given commandment to bless, and he hath blessed, and we cannot reverse it; he hath not seen iniquity in Jacob, and he hath not seen perverseness in Israel; the Eternal, his God, is with him!" [43]

Anyone does a good deed who removes stumblingblocks out of the way of our feeling and profiting by the witness left by this people. And so, instead of making our Hebrew speakers mean, in their use of the word God, a scientific affirmation which never entered into their heads, and about which many will dispute, let us content ourselves with making them mean, as a matter of scientific fact and experience, what they really did mean as such, and what is unchallengeable. Let us put into their "Eternal" and "God" no more science than they did—*the enduring power, not ourselves, which makes for righteousness*. They meant more by these names, but they meant this; and this they grasped fully. And the sense which this will give us for their words is at least solid; so that we may find it of use as a guide to steady us, and to give us a constant clue in following what they say.

And is it so unworthy? It is true, unless we can fill it with as much feeling as they did, the mere possessing it will not carry us far. But matters are not at all mended by taking their language of approximate figure and turning it into the language of scientific definition; or by crediting them with our own dubious science, deduced from metaphysical ideas which they never had. A better way than this, surely, is to take their fact of experience, to keep it steadily for our basis in using their language, and to see whether from using their

[43] Numbers 23:20–21.

language with the ground of this real and firm sense to it, as they themselves did, somewhat of their feeling, too, may not grow upon us. At least we shall know what we are saying; and that what we are saying is true, however inadequate.

But is this confessed inadequateness of our speech, concerning that which we will not call by the negative name of the unknown and unknowable, but rather by the name of the unexplored and inexpressible, and of which the Hebrews themselves said: *It is more high than heaven what canst thou do? deeper than hell, what canst thou know?* [44] —is this reservedness of affirmation about God less worthy of him, than the astounding particularity and licence of affirmation of our dogmatists, as if he were a man in the next street? Nay, and nearly all the difficulties which torment theology—as the reconciling God's justice with his mercy, and so on—comes from this licence and particularity; theologians having precisely, as it would often seem, built up a wall first, in order afterwards to run their own heads against it.

This, we say, is what comes of too much talent for abstract reasoning. One cannot help seeing the theory of causation and such things, when one should only see a far simpler matter: the power, the grandeur, the necessity of righteousness. To be sure, a perception of these is at the bottom of popular religion, underneath all the extravagances theologians have taught people to utter, and makes the whole value of it. For the sake of this true practical perception one might be quite content to leave at rest a matter where practice, after all, is everything, and theory nothing. Only, when religion is called in question because of the extravagances of theology being passed off as religion, one disengages and helps religion by showing their utter delusiveness. . . .

[44] Job 11:8.

Chapter II

Aberglaube Invading

1

When people ask for our attention because of what has passed, they say, "in the Council of the Trinity," and been promulgated, for our direction, by "a Personal First Cause, the moral and intelligent Governor of the universe," it is certainly open to any man to refuse to hear them, on the plea that the very thing they start with they have no means of proving. And we see that many do so refuse their attention; and that the breach there is, for instance, between popular religion and what is called *science*, comes from this cause. But it is altogether different when people ask for our attention on the strength of this other first principle: "To righteousness belongs happiness"; or this: "There is an enduring power, not ourselves, which makes for righteousness." The more we meditate on this starting ground of theirs, the more we shall find that there is solidity in it, and the more we shall be inclined to go along with them and to see what will come of it. . . .

Let us fix firmly in our minds the connexion of ideas which was ever present to the spirit of the Hebrew people. *In the way of righteousness is life, and in the pathway thereof is no death; as righteousness tendeth to life, so he that pursueth evil, pursueth it to his own death; as the whirlwind passeth, so is the wicked no more, but the righteous is an everlasting foundation*—here is the ground-idea [1] Yet there are continual momentary suggestions which make for gratifying our apparent self, for unrighteousness; never-

[1] Proverbs 12:28; 11:19; 10:25.

theless, what makes for our real self, for righteousness, is
lasting, and holds good in the end. Therefore: *Trust in the
Eternal with all thine heart, and lean not unto thine own
understanding; there is no wisdom, nor understanding, nor
counsel against the Eternal; there is a way that seemeth
right unto a man, but the end thereof are the ways of death;
there are many devices in a man's heart, nevertheless, the
counsel of the Eternal, that shall stand.*[2] To follow this
counsel of the Eternal is the only true wisdom and understanding: *The fear of the Eternal, that is wisdom, and to
depart from evil, that is understanding.*[3] It is also happiness: *Blessed is everyone that feareth the Eternal, that
walketh in his ways; happy shall he be, and it shall be well
with him!*[4] *O taste and see how gracious the Eternal is!
Blessed is the man that trusteth in him.*[5] *Blessed is the man
whose delight is in the law of the Eternal; his leaf shall not
wither, and whatsoever he doeth, it shall prosper.*[6] And the
more a man walks in this way of righteousness, the more he
feels himself borne by a power not his own: *Not by might
and not by power, but by my spirit, saith the Eternal.*[7] *O
Eternal, I know that the way of man is not in himself! all
things come of thee; in thy light do we see light; man's
goings are of the Eternal; the Eternal ordereth a good man's
going, and maketh his way acceptable to himself.*[8] But man
feels, too, how far he always is from fulfilling or even from
fully perceiving this true law of his being, these indications
of the Eternal, the way of righteousness. He says, and must
say: *I am a stranger upon earth, Oh, hide not thy commandments from me! Enter not into judgment with thy servant,
O Eternal, for in thy sight shall no man living be justified!*[9]
Nevertheless, as a man holds on to practice as well as he can,

[2] Proverbs 3:5; 21:30; 14:12; 19:21.
[3] Job 28:28.   [4] Psalms 128:1, 2.
[5] Psalms 34:8.   [6] Psalms 1:1, 2, 3.
[7] Zachariah 4:6.
[8] Jeremiah 10:23; I Chronicles 29:14; Psalms 36:9; Proverbs 20:24;
Psalms 37:23.   [9] Psalms 119:19; 143:2.

and avoids, at any rate, "presumptuous sins," courses he can clearly see to be wrong, films fall away from his eyes, the indications of the Eternal come out more and more fully, we are cleansed from faults which were hitherto secret to us: *Examine me, O God, and prove me, try out my reins and my heart; look well if there be any way of wickedness in me, and lead me in the way everlasting!* [10] *O cleanse thou me from my secret faults! thou hast tried me and shalt find nothing.*[11] And the more we thus get to keep innocency, the more we wonderfully find joy and peace: *O how plentiful is thy goodness which thou hast laid up for them that fear thee! thou shalt hide them in the secret of thy presence from the provoking of men.*[12] *Thou wilt show me the path of life, in thy presence is the fulness of joy, at thy right hand there are pleasures for evermore.*[13] More and more this dwelling on the joy and peace from righteousness, and on the power which makes for righteousness, becomes a man's consolation and refuge. *Thou art my hiding place, thou shalt preserve me from trouble; if my delight had not been in thy law, I should have perished in my trouble.*[14] *In the day of my trouble I sought the Eternal; a refuge from the storm, a shadow from the heat!* [15] *O lead me to the rock that is higher than I!* [16] *The name of the Eternal is as a strong tower, the righteous runneth into it and is safe.*[17] And the more we experience this shelter, the more we come to feel that it is protecting even to tenderness: *Like as a father pitieth his own children, even so is the Eternal merciful unto them that fear him.*[18] Nay, every other support, we at last find, every other attachment may fail us; this alone fails not: *Can a woman forget her sucking child, that she should not have compassion on the son of her womb? Yea, they may forget, yet will I not forget thee!* [19]

[10] Psalms 26:2; 139:24.
[11] Psalms 19:12; 17:3.
[12] Psalms 31: 19, 20.
[13] Psalms 16:11.
[14] Psalms 32:7; 119:92.
[15] Psalms 77:2; Isaiah 25:4.
[16] Psalms 61:2.
[17] Proverbs 18:10.
[18] Psalms 103:13.
[19] Isaiah 49:15.

All this, we say, rests originally upon the simple but solid experience: "Conduct brings *happiness*," or, "Righteousness tendeth to *life*." [20] And, by making it again rest there, we bring out in a new but most real and sure way its truth and its power.

Israel questions that the righteous is an everlasting foundation

For it has not always continued to rest there, and in popular religion now, as we manifestly see, it rests there no longer. It is important to follow the way in which this change gradually happened, and the thing ceased to rest there. Israel's original perception was true: *Righteousness tendeth to life!* [21] It was true, that the workers of righteousness have *a covenant with the Eternal*, that their work shall be blessed and blessing, and shall endure for ever. But what apparent contradictions was this true original perception destined to meet with! What vast delays, at any rate, were to be interposed before its truth could become manifest! And how instructively the successive documents of the Bible, which popular religion treats as if it were all of one piece, one time, and one mind, bring out the effect on Israel of these delays and contradictions! What a distance between the eighteenth Psalm and the eighty-ninth; between the Book of Proverbs and the Book of Ecclesiastes! A time some thousand years before Christ, the golden age of Israel, is the date to which the eighteenth Psalm and the chief part of the Book of Proverbs belong. This is the time in which the sense of the necessary connexion between righteousness and happiness appears with its full simplicity and force. *The righteous shall be recompensed in the earth, much more the wicked and the sinner!* is the constant burden of the Book of Proverbs; *the evil bow before the good, and the wicked at the gates of the righteous!* [22] And David, in the eighteenth

20 Proverbs 11:19.   21 Proverbs 11:19.
22 Proverbs 11:31; 14:19.

Psalm, expresses his conviction of the intimate dependence of happiness upon conduct, in terms which, though they are without certain crudity, are yet far more edifying in their truth and naturalness than those morbid sentimentalities of Protestantism about man's natural vileness and Christ's imputed righteousness, to which they are diametrically opposed. "I have kept the ways of the Eternal," he says; "I was also upright before him, and I kept myself from mine iniquity; *therefore* hath the Eternal rewarded me according to my righteousness, according to the cleanness of my hands hath he recompensed me; great prosperity showeth he unto his king, and showeth loving-kindness unto David his anointed, and unto his seed for evermore." That may be called a classic passage for the *covenant* Israel always thinks and speaks of as made by God with his servant David, Israel's second founder. And this covenant was but a renewal of the covenant made with Israel's first founder, God's servant Abraham, that "righteousness shall inherit a blessing," and that *"in thy seed all nations of the earth shall be blessed."* [23]

But what a change in the eighty-ninth Psalm, a few hundred years later! "Eternal, where are thy former loving-kindnesses which thou swarest unto David? thou hast abhorred and forsaken thine anointed, thou hast made void the covenant; O remember how short my time is!" [24] *"The righteous shall be recompensed in the earth!"* the speaker means; "my death is near, and death ends all; where, Eternal, is thy promise?"

Most remarkable, indeed, is the inward travail to which, in the six hundred years that followed the age of David and Solomon, the many and rude shocks befalling Israel's fundamental idea, *Righteousness tendeth to life and he that pursueth evil pursueth it to his own death*, gave occasion. "Wherefore do the wicked live," asks Job, "become old, yea, are mighty in power? their houses are safe

[23] I Peter 3:9; Genesis 26:4.   [24] Psalms 89:49, 38, 39, 47.

from fear, neither is the rod of God upon them." [25] Job
himself is righteous, and yet: "On mine eyelids is the shadow
of death, not for any injustice in mine hands." [26] All
through the Book of Job the question, how this can be, is
over and over again asked and never answered; inadequate
solutions are offered and repelled, but an adequate solution
is never reached. The only solution reached is that of silence
before the insoluble: "I will lay mine hand upon my
mouth." [27] The two perceptions, *Righteousness tendeth to
life*, and, *The ungodly prosper in the world*, are left con-
fronting one another like Kantian antinomies.[28] "*The
earth is given unto the hand of the wicked!*" and yet: "*The
counsel of the wicked is far from me*; *God rewardeth him,
and he shall know it!*" [29] And this last, the original perception, remains indestructible. The Book of Ecclesiastes has
been called sceptical, epicurean; it is certainly without the
glow and hope which animate the Bible in general. It belongs, probably, to the fourth century before Christ, to the
latter and worse days of the Persian power; with difficulties
pressing the Jewish community on all sides, with a Persian
governor lording it in Jerusalem, with resources light and
taxes heavy, with the cancer of poverty eating into the mass
of the people, with the rich estranged from the poor and
from the national traditions, with the priesthood slack, in-
sincere and worthless. Composed under such circumstances,
the book has been said, and with justice, to breathe *resignation at the grave of Israel*. Its author sees "the tears of the
oppressed, and they had no comforter, and on the side of
their oppressors there was power; wherefore I praised the
dead which are already dead more than the living which are
yet alive." [30] He sees "all things come alike to all, there is
one event to the righteous and to the wicked." [31] Attempts

[25] Job 21:7, 9.
[27] Job 40:4.
[29] Job 9:24; 21:16, 19.
[31] Ecclesiastes 9:2.

[26] Job 16:16–17.
[28] Proverbs 11:19; Psalms 73:12.
[30] Ecclesiastes 4:1, 2.

at a philosophic indifference appear, at a sceptical suspension of judgment, at an easy *ne quid nimis*: "Be not righteous overmuch, neither make thyself overwise! why shouldst thou destroy thyself?" [32] Vain attempts, even at a moment which favoured them! shows of scepticism, vanishing as soon as uttered before the intractable conscientiousness of Israel. For the Preacher makes answer against himself: "Though a sinner do evil a hundred times and his days be prolonged, yet surely I know that it shall be well with them that fear God; but it shall not be well with the wicked, because he feareth not before God." [33]

Israel's indestructible faith maintained

Malachi, probably almost contemporary with the Preacher, felt the pressure of the same circumstances, had the same occasions of despondency. All around him people were saying: "Every one that doeth evil is good in the sight of the Eternal, and he delighteth in them; where is the God of judgment? it is vain to serve God, and what profit is it that we have kept his ordinance?" [34] What a change from the clear certitude of the golden age: "As the whirlwind passeth, so is the wicked no more; but the righteous is an everlasting foundation!" [35] But yet, with all the certitude of this happier past, Malachi answers on behalf of the Eternal: "Unto you that fear my name shall the sun of righteousness arise with healing in his wings!" [36]

Many there were, no doubt, who had lost all living sense that the promises were made to *righteousness*; who took them mechanically, as made to them and assured to them because they were the seed of Abraham, because they were, in St. Paul's words: "Israelites, to whom pertain the adoption and the glory and the covenants and the giving of the law and the service of God, and whose are the fathers." [37]

[32] Ecclesiastes 7:16.
[33] Ecclesiastes 8:12, 13.
[34] Malachi 2:17; 3:14.
[35] Proverbs 10:25.
[36] Malachi 4:2.
[37] Romans 9:45.

These people were perplexed and indignant when the privileged seed became unprosperous; and they looked for some great change to be wrought in the fallen fortunes of Israel, wrought miraculously and materially. And these were, no doubt, the great majority; and of the mass of Jewish expectation concerning the future they stamped the character. With them, however, our interest does not so much lie; it lies rather with the prophets and those whom the prophets represent. It lies with the continued depositaries of the original revelation to Israel, *Righteousness tendeth to life*; who saw clearly enough that the promises were to *righteousness,* and that what *tendeth to life* was not the seed of Abraham taken in itself, but *righteousness.* With this minority, and with its noble representatives the prophets, our present interest lies; the further development of their conviction about righteousness is what it here imports us to trace. An indestructible faith that *the righteous is an everlasting foundation* they had; yet they too, as we have seen, could not but notice, as time went on, many things which seemed apparently to contradict this their belief. In private life, there was the frequent prosperity of the sinner. In the life of nations, there was the rise and power of the great unrighteous kingdoms of the heathen, the unsuccessfulness of Israel; although Israel was undoubtedly, as compared with the heathen, the depositary and upholder of the idea of righteousness. Therefore prophets and righteous men also, like the unspiritual crowd, could not but look ardently and expectantly to the future, to some great change and redress in store.

At the same time, although their experience that the righteous were often afflicted, and the wicked often prosperous, could not but perplex pious Hebrews; although their conscience felt, and could not but feel, that, compared with the other nations with whom they came in contact, they themselves and their fathers had a concern for righteousness, and an unremitting sense of its necessity, which put them in covenant with the Eternal who makes for righteousness, and which rendered the triumph of other nations over them a triumph of people who cared little for righteousness over people who cared for it much, and a cause of perplexity, therefore, to men's trust in the Eternal—though their conscience told them this, yet of their own shortcomings and perversities it told them louder still, and that their sins had in truth been enough to break their covenant with the Eternal a thousand times over, and to bring justly upon them all the miseries they suffered. To enable them to meet the terrible day, when the Eternal would avenge him of his enemies and make up his jewels, they themselves needed, they knew, the voice of a second Elijah, a change of the inner man, *repentance*.[38]

2

And then, with Malachi's testimony on its lips to the truth of Israel's ruling idea, *Righteousness tendeth to life!* died prophecy. Through some four hundred years the mind of Israel revolved those wonderful utterances, which, even now, on the ear of even those who only half understand them and who do not at all believe them, strike with such strange, incomparable power—the promises of prophecy. Through four hundred years, amid distress and humiliation, the Hebrew race pondered those magnificent assurances that *"the Eternal's arm is not shortened,"* that *"righteousness shall be for ever,"* [39] and that the future would prove this, even if the present did not. . . .

The invasion of extra-belief

The prophets themselves, speaking when the ruin of their country was impending, or soon after it had happened, had for the most part had in prospect the actual restoration of Jerusalem, the submission of the nations around, and the empire of David and Solomon renewed. But as time went

38 Malachi 3:17; 4:5.   39 Isaiah 59:1; 51:8.

on, and Israel's return from captivity and resettlement of
Jerusalem by no means answered his glowing anticipations
from them, these anticipations had more and more a construction put upon them which set at defiance the unworth-
iness and infelicities of the actual present, which filled up
what prophecy left in outline, and which embraced the
world. The Hebrew Amos, of the eighth century before
Christ, promises to his hearers a recovery from their ruin in
which they *shall possess the remnant of Edom;* the Greek or
Aramaic Amos of the Christian era, whose words St. James
produces in the conference at Jerusalem, promises a recovery for Israel in which *the residue of men shall seek the
Eternal.*[40] This is but a specimen of what went forward on
a large scale. The redeemer, whom the unknown prophet of
the captivity foretold to Zion,[41] has, a few hundred years
later, for the writer whom we call Daniel and for his con-
temporaries, become the miraculous agent of Israel's new
restoration, the heaven-sent executor of the Eternal's judgment, and the bringer-in of the kingdom of righteousness—
the Messiah, in short, of our popular religion. "One like the
Son of Man came with the clouds of heaven, and came to
the Ancient of Days, and there was given him dominion and
glory, and a kingdom, that all people, nations, and languages should serve him; and the kingdom and dominion
shall be given to the people of the saints of the Most
High.[42] An impartial criticism will hardly find in the Old
Testament writers before the times of the Maccabees (and
certainly not in the passages usually quoted to prove it) the
set doctrine of the immortality of the soul or of the resurrection of the dead. But by the time of the Maccabees, when
this passage of the Book of Daniel was written, in the second
century before Christ, the Jews have undoubtedly become
familiar, not indeed with the idea of the immortality of the
soul as philosophers like Plato conceived it, but with the

[40] Amos 9:12; Acts 15:17.   [41] Isaiah 59:20.
[42] Daniel 7:13, 14, 27.

notion of a resurrection of the dead to take their trial for acceptance or rejection in the Most High's judgment and kingdom.

To this, then, has swelled Israel's original and fruitful thesis—*Righteousness tendeth to life! as the whirlwind passeth, so is the wicked no more, but the righteous is an everlasting foundation!* [43] The phantasmagories of more prodigal and wild imaginations have mingled with the product of Israel's own austere spirit; Babylon, Persia, Egypt, even Greece, have left their trace there; but the unchangeable substructure remains, and on that substructure is everything built which comes after.

In one sense, the lofty Messianic ideas of "the great and notable day of the Eternal," "the consolation of Israel," "the restitution of all things," [44] are even more important than the solid but humbler idea, *righteousness tendeth to life*, out of which they arose. In another sense they are much less important. They are more important, because they are the development of this idea and prove its strength. It might have been crushed and baffled by the falsification events seemed to delight in giving it; that instead of being crushed and baffled, it took this magnificent flight, shows its innate power. And they also in a wonderful manner attract emotion to the ideas of conduct and morality, attract it to them and combine it with them. On the other hand, the idea that *righteousness tendeth to life* has a firm, experimental ground, which the Messianic ideas have not. And the day comes when the possession of such a ground is invaluable.

That the spirit of man should entertain hopes and anticipations, beyond what it actually knows and can verify, is quite natural. Human life could not have the scope, and depth, and progress it has, were this otherwise. It is natural, too, to make these hopes and anticipations give in their turn support to the simple and humble experience which was

[43] Proverbs 11:19; 10:25.
[44] Acts 2:20; Luke 2:25; Acts 3:21.

their original ground. Israel, therefore, who originally followed righteousness because he felt that it tended to life, might and did naturally come at last to follow it because it would enable him to stand before the Son of Man at his coming, and to share in the triumph of the saints of the Most High.

But this latter belief has not the same character as the belief which it is thus set to confirm. It is a kind of fairy-tale, which a man tells himself, which no one, we grant, can prove impossible to turn out true, but which no one also can prove certain to turn out true. It is exactly what is expressed by the German word "Aberglaube," *extra-belief,* belief beyond what is certain and verifiable. Our word "superstition" had by its derivation this same meaning, but it has come to be used in a merely bad sense, and to mean a childish and craven religiosity. With the German word it is not so; therefore Goethe can say with propriety and truth: *"Aberglaube* is the poetry of life—*der Aberglaube ist die Poesie des Lebens."* It is so. *Extra-belief,* that which we hope, augur, imagine, is the poetry of life, and has the rights of poetry. But it is not science; and yet it tends always to imagine itself science, to substitute itself for science, to make itself the ground of the very science out of which it has grown. The Messianic ideas, which were the poetry of life to Israel in the age when Jesus Christ came, did this; and it is the more important to mark that they did it, because similar ideas have so signally done the same thing with popular Christianity.

Chapter III

Religion New-Given

1

Jesus Christ was undoubtedly the very last sort of Messiah that the Jews expected. Christian theologians say confidently that the characters of humility, obscureness, and depression, were commonly attributed to the Jewish Messiah; and even Bishop Butler, in general the most severely exact of writers, gives countenance to this error. What is true is, that we find these characters attributed to *some one* by the prophets; that *we* attribute them to Jesus Christ; that Jesus is for us the Messiah, and that Jesus they suit. But for the prophets themselves, and for the Jews who heard and read them, these characters of lowliness and depression belonged to God's chastened servant, the idealised Israel. When Israel had been purged and renewed by these, the Messiah was to appear; but with glory and power for his attributes, not humility and weakness. . . . To find in Jesus the genuine Jewish Messiah, or to find in him the Son of Man of Daniel, one coming with the clouds of heaven and having universal dominion given him, must certainly, to a Jew, have been extremely difficult.

Nevertheless, there is undoubtedly in the Old Testament the germ of Christianity. In developing this germ lay the future of righteousness itself, of Israel's primary and immortal concern; and the incomparable greatness of the religion founded by Jesus Christ comes from his having developed it. Jesus Christ is not the Messiah to whom the hopes of his nation pointed; and yet Christendom with perfect justice has made him the Messiah, because he alone took, when his nation was on another and a false tack, a way obscurely indicated in the Old Testament, and the one only possible and successful way, for the accomplishment of the Messiah's function—*to bring in everlasting righteousness.*[1] Let us see how this was so. . . .

Israel's conduct becomes external and mechanical

We have seen how, in its intuition of God—of that "not ourselves" of which all mankind form some conception or other—*as the Eternal that makes for righteousness,* the Hebrew race found the revelation needed to breathe emotion into the laws of morality, and to make morality religion. This revelation is the capital fact of the Old Testament, and the source of its grandeur and power. But it is evident that this revelation lost, as time went on, its nearness and clearness; and that for the mass of the Hebrews their God came to be a mere magnified and non-natural man, like the God of our popular religion now, who has commanded certain courses of conduct and attached certain sanctions to them.

And though prophets and righteous men, among the Hebrews, might preserve always the immediate and truer apprehension of their God *as the Eternal who makes for righteousness,* they in vain tried to communicate this apprehension to the mass of their countrymen. They had, indeed, a special difficulty to contend with in communicating it; and the difficulty was this. Those courses of conduct, which Israel's intuition of the Eternal had originally touched with emotion and made religion, lay chiefly, we have seen, in the line of national and social duties. By reason of the stage of their own growth and the world's, at which this revelation found the Hebrews, the thing could not well be otherwise. And national and social duties are peculiarly capable of a mechanical exterior performance, in which the heart has no share. One may observe rites and ceremonies, hate idolatry, abstain from murder and theft and false witness, and yet

[1] Daniel 9:24.

have one's inward thoughts bad, callous, and disordered. Then even the admitted duties themselves come to be ill-discharged or set at nought, because the emotion which was the only certain security for their good discharge is wanting. The very power of religion, as we have seen, lies in its bringing *emotion* to bear on our rules of conduct, and thus making us care for them so much, consider them so deeply and reverentially, that we surmount the great practical difficulty of acting in obedience to them, and follow them heartily and easily. Therefore the Israelites, when they lost their primary intuition and the deep feeling which went with it, were perpetually idolatrous, perpetually slack or niggardly in the service of Jehovah, perpetually violators of judgment and justice.

The prophets earnestly reminded their nation of the superiority of judgment and justice to any exterior ceremony like sacrifice. But judgment and justice themselves, as Israel in general conceived them, have something exterior in them; now, what was wanted was more *inwardness*, and *feeling*. This was given by adding *mercy* and *humbleness* to judgment and justice. Mercy and humbleness are something inward, they are affections of the heart. And even in the Proverbs these appear: "The *merciful* man doeth good to his own soul"; "He that hath *mercy* on the poor, happy is he"; "Honour shall uphold the *humble* in spirit"; "When pride cometh, shame cometh, but with the lowly is wisdom." [2] And the prophet Micah asked his nation: "What doth the Eternal require of thee, but to do justly, and to love *mercy*, and to walk *humbly* with thy God?"—adding mercy and humility to the old judgment and justice.[3] But a farther development is given to humbleness, when the second Isaiah adds contrition to it: "I" (the Eternal) "dwell with him that is of a *contrite* and humble spirit";[4] or when the Psalmist says, "The sacrifices of God are a

[2] Proverbs 11:17; 14:21; 29:23; 11:2.
[3] Micah 6:8.   [4] Isaiah 57:15.

broken spirit; a *broken* and a *contrite heart,* O God, thou wilt not despise!" [5]

This is *personal religion*; religion consisting in the inward feeling and disposition of the individual himself, rather than in the performance of outward acts towards religion or society. It is the essence of Christianity, it is what the Jews needed, it is the line in which their religion was ripe for development. And it *appears* in the Old Testament. Still, in the Old Testament it by no means comes out fully. The leaning, there, is to make religion social rather than personal, an affair of outward duties rather than of inward dispositions. Soon after the very words we have just quoted from him, the second Isaiah adds: "If thou take away from the midst of thee the yoke, the putting forth of the finger and speaking vanity, and if thou draw out thy soul to the hungry, and satisfy the afflicted soul, then shall thy light rise in obscurity and thy darkness be as the noon-day, and the Eternal shall guide thee continually and make fat thy bones." [6] This stands, or at least appears to stand, as a full description of righteousness; and as such, it is unsatisfying.

2

Jesus's conception of righteousness

What was wanted, then, was a fuller description of righteousness. Now, it is clear that righteousness, the central object of Israel's concern, was the central object of Jesus Christ's concern also. Of the development and of the cardinal points of his teaching we shall have to speak more at length by-and-by; all we have to do here is to pass them in a rapid preliminary review. Israel had said: "To him that ordereth his conversation right shall be shown the salvation of God." [7] And Jesus said: "Except your righteousness ex-

[5] Psalms 51:17.
[6] Isaiah 58:9–11.
[7] Psalms 50:23.

ceed the righteousness of the Scribes and Pharisees"—that is, of the very people who then passed for caring most about righteousness and practising it most rigidly—"ye shall in no wise enter into the kingdom of heaven." [8] But righteousness had by Jesus Christ's time lost, in great measure, the mighty impulse which emotion gives; and in losing this, had lost also the mighty sanction which happiness gives. "The whole head was sick and the whole heart faint";[9] the glad and immediate sense of being in the right way, in the way of peace, was gone; the sense of being wrong and astray, of sin, and of helplessness under sin, was oppressive. The thing was, by giving a fuller idea of righteousness, to re-apply *emotion* to it, and by thus re-applying emotion, to disperse the feeling of being amiss and helpless, to give the sense of being right and effective; to restore, in short, to righteousness the sanction of *happiness*.

But this could only be done by attending to that inward world of feelings and dispositions which Judaism had too much neglected. The first need, therefore, for Israel at that time, was to make religion cease to be mainly a national and social matter, and become mainly a personal matter. "Thou blind Pharisee, cleanse first the *inside* of the cup, that the outside may be clean also!" [10]—this was the very ground-principle in Jesus Christ's teaching. Instead of attending so much to your outward acts, attend, he said, first of all to your inward thoughts, to the state of your heart and feelings. This doctrine has perhaps been overstrained and misapplied by certain people since; but it was the lesson which at that time was above all needed. It is a great progress beyond even that advanced maxim of pious Jews: "To do justice and judgment is more acceptable than sacrifice." [11] For to do justice and judgment is still, as we have remarked, something external, and may leave the feelings untouched, uncleared, dead. What was wanted was to

8 Matthew 5:20. 9 Isaiah 1:5.
10 Matthew 23:26. 11 Proverbs 21:3.

plough up, clear, and quicken the feelings themselves. And this is what Jesus Christ did. . . .

Jesus Christ's new and different way of putting things was the secret of his succeeding where the prophets failed. And this new way he had of putting things is what is indicated by the expression *epieikeia*—an expression best rendered, as I have elsewhere said,[12] by the phrase: "sweet reasonableness." For that which is *epieikes* is that which has an air of truth and likelihood; and that which has an air of truth and likelihood is prepossessing. Now, never were there utterances concerning conduct and righteousness—Israel's master-concern, and the master-topic of the New Testament as well as of the Old—which so carried with them an air of consummate truth and likelihood as Jesus Christ's did; and never, therefore, were any utterances so irresistibly prepossessing. He put things in such a way that his hearer was led to take each rule or fact of conduct by its inward side, its effect on the heart and character; then the reason of the thing, the meaning of what had been mere matter of blind rule, flashed upon him. The hearer could distinguish between what was only ceremony, and what was *conduct*; and the hardest rule of conduct came to appear to him infinitely reasonable and natural, and therefore infinitely prepossessing. A return upon themselves, and a consequent intuition of the truth and reason of the matter of conduct in question, gave men for right action the clearness, spirit, energy, happiness, they had lost.

Jesus's new lessons

This power of returning upon themselves, and seeing by a flash the truth and reason of things, his disciples learnt of Jesus. They learnt too, from observing him and his example, much which, without perhaps any conscious process of being apprehended in its reason, was discerned instinctively to be true and life-giving as soon as it was recommended in

[12] *St. Paul and Protestantism.*

Christ's words and illustrated by Christ's example. Two lessons in particular they learnt in this way, and added them to the great lesson of self-examination and appeal to the inner man, with which they started. *"Whoever will come after me, let him renounce himself and take up his cross daily and follow me! he that will save his life shall lose it, he that will lose his life shall save it."* [13] This was one of the two. *"Learn of me that I am mild and lowly in heart, and ye shall find rest unto your souls!"* [14] was the other. Jesus made his followers first look within and examine themselves; he made them feel that they had a best and real self as opposed to their ordinary and apparent one, and that their happiness depended on saving this best self from being overborne. Then *to find his own soul,* [15] his true and permanent self, became set up in man's view as his chief concern, as the secret of happiness; and so it really is. "How is a man advantaged if he gain the whole world and forfeit *himself?"* [16]—was the searching question which Jesus made men ask themselves. And by recommending, and still more by himself exemplifying in his own practice, by showing active in himself, with the most prepossessing pureness, clearness and beauty, the two qualities by which our ordinary self is indeed most essentially counteracted, *self-renounce-ment* and *mildness,* he made his followers feel that in these qualities lay the secret of their best self; that to attain them was in the highest degree requisite and natural, and that a man's whole happiness depended upon it.

Self-examination, self-renouncement, and mildness, were, therefore, the great means by which Jesus Christ renewed righteousness and religion. All these means are indicated in the Old Testament: *God requireth truth in the inward parts! Not doing thine own ways, nor finding thine own pleasure! Seek meekness!* [17] But how far more strongly

---

[13] Luke 9:23–24.   [14] Matthew 11:29.
[15] Matthew 16:25.   [16] Luke 9:25.
[17] Psalms 51:6; Isaiah 58:13; Zephaniah 2:3.

are they forced upon the attention in the New Testament, and set up clearly as the central mark for our endeavours! *Thou blind Pharisee, cleanse first the inside of the cup that the outside may be clean also!* [18] *Whoever will come after me, let him renounce himself and take up his cross daily and follow me!* [19] *Learn of me that I am mild and lowly in heart, and ye shall find rest unto your souls!* [20] So that, although personal religion is clearly recommended in the Old Testament, nevertheless these injunctions of the New Testament effect so much more for the extrication and establishment of personal religion than the general exhortations in the Old to *offer the sacrifice of righteousness, to do judgment,*[21] that, comparatively with the Old, the New Testament may be said to have really founded inward personal religion. While the Old Testament says: *Attend to conduct!* the New Testament says: *Attend to the feelings and dispositions whence conduct proceeds!* And as attending to conduct had very much degenerated into deadness and formality, attending to the *springs* of conduct was a revelation, a revival of intuitive and fresh perceptions, a touching of morals with emotion, a discovering of religion, similar to that which had been effected when Israel, struck with the abiding power not of man's causing which makes for righteousness, and filled with joy and awe by it, had in the old days named God *the Eternal.* Man came under a new dispensation, and made with God a second covenant. . . .

3

The coming of new Aberglaube

And thus was the great doctrine of the Old Testament: *To righteousness belongs happiness!* made a true and potent word again. Jesus Christ was the Messiah to restore the

[18] Matthew 23:26.   [19] Luke 9:23.
[20] Matthew 11:29.   [21] Psalms 4:5; Isaiah 56:1.

all things of Israel [22]—righteousness, and happiness with righteousness; to bring light and recovery after long days of darkness and ruin, and to make good the belief written on Israel's heart: *The righteous is an everlasting foundation!* [23] But we have seen how in the hopes of the nation and in the promises of prophecy this true and vital belief of Israel was mixed with a quantity of what we have called *Aberglaube* or extra-belief, adding all manner of shape and circumstance to the original thought. The kingdom of David and Solomon was to be restored on a grander scale, the enemies of Israel were to lick the dust, kings were to bring gifts; there was to be the Son of Man coming in the clouds, judgment given to the saints of the Most High, and an eternal reign of the saints afterwards.

Now, most of this has a poetical value, some of it has a moral value. All of it is, in truth, a testimony to the strength of Israel's idea of righteousness. For the order of its growth is, as we have seen, this: *"To righteousness belongs happiness*; but this sure rule is often broken in the state of things which now is; there must, therefore, be in store for us, in the future, a state of things where it will hold good." But none of it has a scientific value, a certitude arising from proof and experience. And indeed it cannot have this, for it professes to be an anticipation of a state of things not yet actually experienced.

But human nature is such, that the mind easily dwells on an anticipation of this kind until we come to forget the order in which it arose, place it first when it is by rights second, and make it support that by which it is in truth supported. And so there had come to be many Israelites—most likely they were the great majority of their nation—who supposed that righteousness was to be followed, not out of thankful self-surrender to "the Eternal who loveth righteousness," [24] but because the Ancient of Days was to sit

[22] Matthew 17:11; Acts 3:21.   [23] Proverbs 10:25.
[24] Psalms 11:7.

before long, and judgment was to be given to the saints, and
they were to possess the kingdom, and from the kingdom
those who did not follow righteousness were to be excluded.
From this way of conceiving religion came naturally the
religious condition of the Jews as Jesus at his coming found
it; and from which, by his new and living way of presenting
the Messiah, he sought to extricate the whole nation, and
did extricate his disciples. He did extricate these, in that he
fixed their thoughts upon himself and upon an ideal of inwardness, mildness, and self-renouncement, instead of a
phantasmagory of outward grandeur and self-assertion. But
at the same time the whole train of an extra-belief, or *Aberglaube,* which had attached itself to Israel's old creed: *The
righteous is an everlasting foundation!* transferred itself to
the new creed brought by Jesus. And there arose, accordingly, a new *Aberglaube* like the old. The mild, inward, self-
renouncing and sacrificed Servant of the Eternal, the new
and better Messiah, was yet, before the present generation
passed, to come on the clouds of heaven in power and glory
like the Messiah of Daniel, to gather by trumpet-call his
elect from the four winds, and to set his apostles on twelve
thrones judging the twelve tribes of Israel. The motive of
Christianity—which was, in truth, that pure souls "knew
the voice" [25] of Jesus as sheep know the voice of their shep-
herd, and felt, after seeing and hearing him, that his doctrine and ideal was what they wanted, that he was "indeed
the saviour of the world" [26]—this simple motive became a
mixed motive, adding to its first contents a vast *extra-belief*
of a phantasmagorical advent of Jesus Christ, a resurrection
and judgment, Christ's adherents glorified, his rejectors
punished everlastingly.

And when the generation, for which this advent was
first fixed, had passed away without it, Christians discovered
by a process of criticism common enough in popular theology, but by which, as Bishop Butler says of a like kind of

process, "anything may be made out of anything"—they discovered that the advent had never really been fixed for that first generation by the writers of the New Testament, but that is was foretold, and certainly in store, for a later time. So the *Aberglaube* was perpetuated, placed out of reach of all practical test, and made stronger than ever. With the multitude, this *Aberglaube*, or extra-belief, inevitably came soon to surpass the original conviction itself in attractiveness and seeming certitude. The future and the miraculous engaged the chief attention of Christians; and, in accordance with this strain of thought, they more and more rested the proof of Christianity, not on its internal evidence, but on prophecy and miracle.

Chapter IV

The Proof from Prophecy

1

"*Aberglaube* is the poetry of life." That men should, by help of their imagination, take short cuts to what they ardently desire, whether the triumph of Israel or the triumph of Christianity, should tell themselves fairy-tales about it, should make these fairy-tales the basis for what is far more sure and solid than the fairy-tales, the desire itself—all this has in it, we repeat, nothing which is not natural, nothing blameable. Nay, the region of our hopes and presentiments extends, as we have also said, far beyond the region of what we can know with certainty. What we reach but by hope and presentiment may yet be true; and he would be a narrow reasoner who denied, for instance, all validity to the idea of immortality, because this idea rests on presentiment mainly, and does not admit of certain demonstration. In religion, above all, *extra-belief* is in itself no matter, assuredly, for blame. The object of religion is conduct; and if a man helps himself in his conduct by taking an object of hope and presentiment as if it were an object of certainty, he may even be said to gain thereby an advantage.

And yet there is always a drawback to a man's advantage in thus treating, when he deals with religion and conduct, what is extra-belief and not certain as if it were matter of certainty, and in making it his ground of action. *He pays for it*. The time comes when he discovers that it is *not* certain; and then the whole certainty of religion seems discredited, and the basis of conduct gone. This danger attends the reliance on prediction and miracle as evidences of Christianity.

73

They have been attacked as a part of the "cheat" or "imposture" of religion and of Christianity. For us, religion is the solidest of realities, and Christianity the greatest and happiest stroke ever yet made for human perfection. Prediction and miracle were attributed to it as its supports because of its grandeur, and because of the awe and admiration which it inspired. Generations of men have helped themselves to hold firmer to it, helped themselves in conduct, by the aid of these supports. "Miracles *prove*," men have said and thought, "that the order of physical nature is not fate, nor a mere material constitution of things, but the subject of a free omnipotent Master. Prophecy fulfilled *proves* that neither fate nor man are masters of the world." [1]

And to take prophecy first. "The conditions," it is said, "which form the true conclusive standard of a prophetic inspiration are these: That the prediction be known to have been promulgated before the event; that the event be such as could not have been foreseen, when it was predicted, by any effort of human reason; and that the event and the prediction correspond together in a clear accomplishment. There are prophecies in Scripture answering to the standard of an absolute proof. Their publication, their fulfilment, their supernatural prescience, are all fully ascertained." [2] On this sort of ground men came to rest the proof of Christianity.

2

The apparent value of proof from prophecy

Now, it may be said, indeed, that a prediction fulfilled, an exhibition of supernatural prescience, proves nothing for or against the truth and necessity of conduct and righteousness. But it must be allowed, notwithstanding, that while

[1] Davison's *Discourses on Prophecy; Discourse* ii, Part 2.
[2] *Discourses* ix and xii.

human nature is what it is, the mass of men are likely to listen more to a teacher of righteousness, if he accompanies his teaching by an exhibition of supernatural prescience. And what were called the "signal predictions" concerning the Christ of popular theology, as they stand in our Bibles, had and have undoubtedly a look of supernatural prescience. The employment of capital letters, and other aids, such as the constant use of the future tense, naturally and innocently adopted by interpreters who were profoundly convinced that Christianity needed these express predictions and that they *must* be in the Bible, enhanced, certainly, this look; but the look, even without these aids, was sufficiently striking.

Yes, that Jacob on his death-bed should two thousand years before Christ have "been enabled," as the phrase is, to foretell to his son Judah that "the sceptre shall not depart from Judah until *Shiloh* (or the Messiah) come, and unto him shall the gathering of the people be," [3] *does* seem, when the explanation is put with it that the Jewish kingdom lasted till the Christian era and then perished, a miracle of prediction in favour of our current Christian theology. That Jeremiah should during the captivity have "been enabled" to foretell, in Jehovah's name: "The days come that I will raise unto David a righteous Branch; in his days Judah shall be saved, and Israel shall dwell safely; and this is his name whereby he shall be called, THE LORD OUR RIGHTEOUSNESS!" [4]—*does* seem a prodigy of prediction in favour of that tenet of the Godhead of the Eternal Son, for which the Bishops of Winchester and Gloucester are so anxious to do something. For unquestionably, in the prophecy here given, the Branch of David, the future Saviour of Israel, who was Jesus Christ, appears to be expressly identified with the Lord God, with Jehovah. Again, that David should say: "The Lord said unto my Lord, Sit thou on my right hand until I make thine enemies thy foot-

---

[3] Genesis 49:10.   [4] Jeremiah 23:5, 6.

stool" [5]—*does* seem a prodigy of prediction to the same effect. And so long as these prophecies stand as they are here given, they no doubt bring to Christianity all the support (and with the mass of mankind this is by no means inconsiderable) which it can derive from the display of supernatural prescience.

Such proofs will not stand criticism

But who will dispute that it more and more becomes known, that these prophecies cannot stand as we have here given them? Manifestly, it more and more becomes known, that the passage from Genesis, with its mysterious *Shiloh* and the gathering of the people to him, is rightly to be rendered as follows: "The pre-eminence shall not depart from Judah *so long as the people resort to Shiloh* (the national sanctuary before Jerusalem was won) ; *and the nations* (the heathen Canaanites) *shall obey him.*" We here purposely leave out of sight any such consideration as that our actual books of the Old Testament came first together through the instrumentality of the house of Judah, and when the destiny of Judah was already traced; and that to say roundly and confidently: "*Jacob was enabled to foretell,* The sceptre shall not depart from Judah," is wholly inadmissible. For this consideration is of force, indeed, but it is a consideration drawn from the rules of literary history and criticism, and not likely to have weight with the mass of mankind. Palpable error and mistranslation are what will have weight with *them*.

And what, then, will they say as they come to know (and do not and must not more and more of them come to know it every day?) that Jeremiah's supposed signal identification of Jesus Christ with the Lord God of Israel: "I will raise to David a righteous Branch, and this is the name whereby he shall be called, *THE LORD OUR RIGHTEOUSNESS*," runs really: "I will raise to David a righteous

[5] Psalms 110:1.

branch; in his days Judah shall be saved and Israel shall dwell safely; and this is the name whereby they shall call themselves: *The Eternal is our righteousness!*" The prophecy thus becomes simply one of the many promises of a successor to David under whom the Hebrew people should trust in the Eternal and follow righteousness; just as the prophecy from Genesis is one of the many prophecies of the enduring continuance of the greatness of Judah. "The Lord said unto my Lord," in like manner—will not people be startled when they find that it ought instead to run as follows: "The Eternal said unto my lord the king"—a simple promise of victory to a royal leader of God's chosen people? . . .

3

It can hardly be gainsaid, that, to a delicate and penetrating criticism, it has long been manifest that the chief *literal* fulfilment by Jesus Christ of things said by the prophets was the fulfilment such as would naturally be given by one who nourished his spirit on the prophets, and on living and acting their words. The great prophecies of Isaiah and Jeremiah are, critics can easily see, not strictly *predictions* at all; and predictions which are strictly meant as such, like those in the Book of Daniel, are an embarrassment to the Bible rather than a main element of it. The "Zeit-Geist," and the mere spread of what is called *enlightenment,* superficial and barren as this often is, will inevitably, before long, make this conviction of criticism a popular opinion, held far and wide. And then, what will be *their* case, who have been so long and sedulously taught to rely on supernatural predictions as a mainstay?

The same must be said of miracles. The substitution of some other proof of Christianity for this accustomed proof is now to be desired most by those who most think Christianity of importance. That old friend of ours on whom we have formerly commented,* who insists upon it that Christianity is and shall be nothing else but this, "that Christ promised Paradise to the saint and threatened the worldly man with hell-fire, *and proved his power to promise and to threaten by rising from the dead and ascending into heaven,*" is certainly not the guide whom lovers of Christianity, if they could discern what it is that he really expects and aims at, and what it is which they themselves really desire, would think it wise to follow.

But the subject of miracles is a very great one; it includes within itself, indeed, the whole question about "supernatural prescience," which meets us when we deal with prophecy. And this great subject requires, in order that we may deal with it properly, some little recapitulation of our original design in this essay, and of the circumstances in which the cause of religion and of the Bible seems to be at this moment placed.

* See *St. Paul and Protestantism*. The friend is Sir James Stephen. Stephen actually denied that Christ's "proofs" were factual events.—*Ed.*

Chapter V

The Proof from Miracles

1

New attacks on the Bible

We have seen that some new treatment or other the
religion of the Bible certainly seems to require, for it is attacked on all sides, and the theologians are not so successful
as one might wish in defending it. One critic* says, that if
these islands had no religion at all it would not enter into
his mind to introduce the religious and ethical idea by the
agency of the Bible. Another, that though certain commonplaces are common to all systems of morality, yet the Bible-
way of enunciating these commonplaces no longer suits us.
And we may rest assured, he adds, that by saying what we
think in some other, more congenial, language, we shall
really be taking the shortest road to discovering the new
doctrines which will satisfy at once our reason and our
imagination. Another critic goes farther still, and calls Bible
religion not only destitute of a modern and congenial way
of stating its commonplaces of morality, but a defacer and
disfigurer of moral treasures which were once in better keeping. The more one studies, the more, says he, one is convinced that the religion which calls itself revealed contains,
in the way of what is good, nothing which is not the inco-
herent and ill-digested residue of the wisdom of the an-
cients. To the same effect the Duke of Somerset†—who has
been affording proof to the world that our aristocratic class
are not, as has been said, inaccessible to ideas and merely

* See Editor's Introduction, p. viii.

† Edward A. Seymour (1804–85), in 1872 published a book
entitled *Christian Theology and Modern Scepticism.—Ed.*

polite, but that they are familiar, on the contrary, with modern criticism of the most advanced kind—the Duke of Somerset finds very much to condemn in the Bible and its teaching; although the soul, he says, has (outside the Bible, apparently) one unassailable fortress to which she may retire—faith in God.

All this seems to threaten to push Bible-religion from the place it has long held in our affections. And even what the most modern criticism of all sometimes does to save it and to set it up again, can hardly be called very flattering to it. For whereas the Hebrew race imagined that to them were committed the oracles of God, and that their God, "the Eternal who loveth righteousness," [1] was the God to whom "every knee shall bow and every tongue shall swear," [2] there now comes M. Émile Burnouf, the accomplished kinsman of the gifted orientalist Éugene Burnouf, and will prove to us in a thick volume[3] that the oracles of God were not committed to a Semitic race at all, but to the Aryan; that the true God is not Israel's God at all, but is "the idea of the absolute" which Israel could never properly master. This "sacred theory of the Aryas," it seems, passed into Palestine from Persia and India, and got possession of the founder of Christianity and of his greatest apostles St. Paul and St. John; becoming more perfect, and returning more and more to its true character of a "transcendent metaphysic," as the doctors of the Christian Church developed it. So that we Christians, who are Aryas, may have the satisfaction of thinking that "the religion of Christ has not come to us from the Semites," and that "it is in the hymns of the Veda, and not in the Bible, that we are to look for the primordial source of our religion." The theory of Christ is accordingly the theory of the Vedic Agni, or *fire*. The Incarnation represents the Vedic solemnity of the production of *fire*, symbol of force of every kind, of all movement, life, and thought.

[1] Psalms 11:7.   [2] Isaiah 45:23.
[3] *La Science des Religions;* Paris, 1872.

The Trinity of Father, Son, and Spirit is the Vedic Trinity of Sun, Fire, and Wind; and God, finally, is "a cosmic unity."

Aryan and Semitic theology

Such speculations almost take away the breath of a mere man of letters. What one is inclined to say of them is this. Undoubtedly these exploits of the Aryan genius are gratifying to us members of the Aryan race. The original God of the Hebrews, M. Burnouf says expressly, "was *not* a cosmic unity"; the religion of the Hebrews "had *not* that transcendent metaphysic which the genius of the Aryas requires"; and, "in passing from the Aryan race to the inferior races, religion underwent a deterioration due to the physical and moral constitution of these races." For religion, it must be remembered, is, in M. Burnouf's view, fundamentally a *science*; "a metaphysical conception, a theory, a synthetic explanation of the universe." Now, "the perfect Arya is capable of a great deal of science; the Semite is inferior to him." As Aryas or Aryans, then, we ought to be pleased at having vindicated the greatness of our race, and having not borrowed a Semitic religion as it stood, but transformed it by importing our own metaphysics into it.

And this seems to harmonise very well with what the Bishops of Winchester and Gloucester say about "doing something for the honour of Our Lord's Godhead," and about "the infinite separation for time and for eternity which is involved in rejecting the Godhead of the Eternal Son, Very God of Very God, Light of Light"; and also with the Athanasian Creed generally, and with what the clergy write to the *Guardian* about "eternal life being unquestionably annexed to a right knowledge of the Godhead." For all these have in view high science and metaphysics, worthy of the Aryas. But to Bible-religion, in the plain sense of the word, it is not flattering; for it throws overboard almost entirely the Old Testament, and makes the essence of the New to consist in an esoteric doctrine not very visible there, but more fully developed outside of it. The metaphysical element is made the fundamental element in religion. . . .

But we, who think that the Old Testament leads surely up to the New, who believe that, indeed, "salvation is of the Jews," [4] and that, for what concerns conduct or righteousness (that is, for what concerns three-fourths of human life) , they and their documents can no more be neglected by whoever would make proficiency in it, than Greece can be neglected by anyone who would make proficiency in art, or Newton's discoveries by whoever would comprehend the world's physical laws—we are naturally not satisfied with this treatment of Israel and the Bible. And admitting that Israel shows no talent for metaphysics, we say that his religious greatness is just this, that he does not found religion on metaphysics, but on moral experience, which is a much simpler matter; and that, ever since the apparition of Israel and the Bible, religion is no longer what, according to M. Burnouf, to our Aryan forefathars in the valley of the Oxus it was—and what perhaps it really was to them—metaphysical theory, but is what Israel had made it.

And what Israel made, and how he made it, we seek to show from the Bible itself. Thus we hope to win for the Bible and its religion, which seem to us so indispensable to the world, an access to many of those who now neglect them. For there is this to be said against M. Burnouf's metaphysics: no one can allege that the Bible has failed to win access for want of metaphysics being applied to it. Metaphysics are just what all our theology runs up into, and our bishops, as we know, are here particularly strong. But we see every day that the making religion into metaphysics is the weakening of religion; now, M. Burnouf makes religion into metaphysics more than ever. Yet evidently the metaphysical method lacks power for laying hold on people, and compelling them to receive the Bible from it; it is felt to be incon-

[4] John 4:22.

clusive as thus employed, and its inconclusiveness tells against the Bible. This is the case with the old metaphysics of our bishops, and it will be the case with M. Burnouf's new metaphysics also. They will be found, we fear, to have an inconclusiveness in their recommendation of Christianity. To very many persons, indeed to the great majority, such a method, in such a matter, *must* be inconclusive. . . .

But the same may now be also said of the popular theology which rests the Bible's authority and the Christian religion on miracle. To a great many persons this is tantamount to stopping their use of the Bible and of the Christian religion; for they have made up their minds that what is popularly called *miracle* never does really happen, and that the belief in it arises out of either ignorance or mistake. To these persons we restore the use of the Bible, if, while showing them that the Bible-language is not scientific, but the language of common speech or of poetry and eloquence, approximative language thrown out at certain great objects of consciousness which it does not pretend to define fully, we convince them at the same time that this language deals with facts of positive experience, most momentous and real.

We have sought to do this for the Old Testament first, and we now seek to do it for the New. But our attempt has in view those who are incredulous about the Bible and inclined to throw it aside, not those who at present receive it on the grounds supplied either by popular theology or by metaphysical theology. . . .

2

*The proneness of men to take miracles
as evidence is passing*

That miracles, when fully believed, are felt by men in general to be a source of authority, it is absurd to deny. One may say, indeed: Suppose I could change the pen with which I write this into a penwiper, I should not thus make what I write any the truer or more convincing. That may be so in reality, but the mass of mankind feel differently. In the judgment of the mass of mankind, could I visibly and undeniably change the pen with which I write this into a pen-wiper, not only would this which I write acquire a claim to be held perfectly true and convincing, but I should even be entitled to affirm, and to be believed in affirming, propositions the most palpably at war with common fact and experience. It is almost impossible to exaggerate the proneness of the human mind to take miracles as evidence, and to seek for miracles as evidence; or the extent to which religion, and religion of a true and admirable kind, has been, and is still, held in connexion with a reliance upon miracles. This reliance will long outlast the reliance on the supernatural prescience of prophecy, for it is not exposed to the same tests. To pick Scripture miracles one by one to pieces is an odious and repulsive task; it is also an unprofitable one, for whatever we may think of the affirmative demonstrations of them, a negative demonstration of them is, from the circumstances of the case, impossible. And yet the human mind is assuredly passing away, however slowly, from this hold of reliance also; and those who make it their stay will more and more find it fail them, will more and more feel themselves disturbed, shaken, distressed, and bewildered.

For it is what we call the *Time-Spirit* which is sapping the proof from miracles—it is the "Zeit-Geist" itself. Whether we attack them, or whether we defend them, does not much matter. The human mind, as its experience widens, is turning away from them. And for this reason: *it sees, as its experience widens, how they arise*. It sees that, under certain circumstances, they always do arise; and that they have not more solidity in one case than another. Under certain circumstances, wherever men are found, there is, as Shakespeare says:

No natural exhalation in the sky,
No scape of nature, no distemper'd day,

No common wind, no customed event,
But they will pluck away his natural cause,
And call them meteors, prodigies, and signs,
Abortives, presages, and tongues of heaven.

Imposture is so far from being the general rule in these cases, that it is the rare exception. Signs and wonders men's minds will have, and they create them honestly and naturally; yet not so but that we can see *how* they create them.

Roman Catholics fancy that Bible-miracles and the miracles of their Church form a class by themselves; Protestants fancy that Bible-miracles, alone, form a class by themselves. This was eminently the posture of mind of the late Archbishop Whately—to hold that all other miracles would turn out to be impostures, or capable of a natural explanation, but that Bible-miracles would stand sifting by a London special jury or by a committee of scientific men. No acuteness can save such notions, as our knowledge widens, from being seen to be mere extravagances, and the Protestant notion is doomed to an earlier ruin than the Catholic. For the Catholic notion admits miracles—so far as Christianity, at least, is concerned—in the mass; the Protestant notion invites to a criticism by which it must before long itself perish. When Stephen was martyred, he looked up into heaven, and saw the glory of God and Jesus standing on the right hand of God. That, says the Protestant, is solid fact. At the martyrdom of St. Fructuosus the Christian servants of the Roman governor, Babylas and Mygdone, saw the heavens open, and the saint and his deacon Eulogius carried up on high with crowns on their heads. That is, says the Protestant, imposture or else illusion. St. Paul hears on his way to Damascus the voice of Jesus say to him: "Saul, Saul, why persecutest thou me?" That is solid fact. The companion of St. Thomas Aquinas hears a voice from the curcifix say to the praying saint: "Thou hast written well of me, Thomas; what recompense dost thou desire?" That is imposture or else illusion. Why? It is impossible to find any criterion by which one of these incidents may establish its claim to a solidity which we refuse to the others.

One of two things must be made out in order to place either the Bible-miracles alone, or the Bible-miracles and the miracles of the Catholic Church with them, in a class by themselves. Either they must be shown to have arisen in a time eminently unfavourable to such a process as Shakespeare describes, to amplification and the production of legend; or they must be shown to be recorded in documents of an eminently historical mode of birth and publication. But surely it is manifest that the Bible-miracles fulfil neither of these conditions. It was said that the waters of the Pamphylian Sea miraculously opened a passage for the army of Alexander the Great. Admiral Beaufort, however, tells us that, "though there are no tides in this part of the Mediterranean, a considerable depression of the sea is caused by long-continued north winds, and Alexander, taking advantage of such a moment, may have dashed on without impediment." [5] And we accept the explanation as a matter of course. But the waters of the Red Sea are said to have miraculously opened a passage for the children of Israel; and we insist on the literal truth of *this* story, and reject natural explanations as impious. . . .

3

There is nothing one would more desire for a person or document one greatly values, than to make them independent of miracles. And with regard to the Old Testament we have done this; for we have shown that the essential matter in the Old Testament is the revelation to Israel of the immeasurable grandeur, the eternal necessity, the priceless blessing of that with which not less than three-fourths of human life is indeed concerned—*righteousness*. And it

[5] Beaufort's *Karamania,* p. 116.

makes no difference to the preciousness of this revelation, whether we believe that the Red Sea miraculously opened a passage to the Israelites, and the walls of Jericho miraculously fell down at the blast of Joshua's trumpet, or that these stories arose in the same way as other stories of the kind. But in the New Testament the essential thing is the revelation of Jesus Christ. For this too, then, if one values it, one's great wish must in like manner be to make it independent of miracle, if miracle is a stay which one perceives, as more and more we are all coming to perceive it, to be not solid.

Bible writers liable to make mistakes

Now, it may look at first sight a strange thing to say, but it is a truth, which we will make abundantly clear as we go on, that one of the very best helps to prepare the way for valuing the Bible and believing in Jesus Christ, is to convince oneself of the liability to mistake in the Bible-writers. Our popular theology supposes that the Old Testament writers were miraculously inspired, and could make no mistakes; that the New Testament writers were miraculously inspired, and could make no mistakes; and that there this miraculous inspiration stopped, and all writers on religion have been liable to make mistakes ever since. It is as if a hand had been put out of the sky presenting us with the Bible, and the rules of criticism which apply to other books did not apply to the Bible. Now, the fatal thing for this supposition is, that its owners stab it to the heart the moment they use any palliation or explaining away, however small, of the literal words of the Bible; and *some* they always use. For instance, it is said in the eighteenth Psalm, that a consuming fire went out of the mouth of God, so that coals were kindled at it. The veriest literalist will cry out: Everyone knows that this is not to be taken literally! The truth is, even *he* knows that *this* is not to be taken literally; but others know that a great deal more is not to be taken literally. He knows very little; but, as far as his little knowledge goes, he gives up his theory, which is, of course, palpably hollow. For indeed it is only by applying to the Bible a criticism, such as it is, that such a man makes out that criticism does not apply to the Bible.

There has grown up an irresistible sense that the belief in miracles was due to man's want of experience, to his ignorance, agitation, and helplessness. And it will not do to stake all truth and value of the Bible upon its having been put out of the sky, upon its being guaranteed by miracles, and upon their being true. If we present the Bible in this fashion, then the cry, *Imposture!* will more and more, in spite of all we can do, gather strength, and the book will be thrown aside more and more.

But when men come to see, that, both in the New Testament and in the Old, what is given us is words *thrown out* at an immense reality not fully or half fully grasped by the writers, but, even thus, able to affect us with indescribable force; when we convince ourselves that, as in the Old Testament we have Israel's inadequate yet inexhaustibly fruitful testimony to *the Eternal that makes for righteousness,* so we have in the New Testament a report inadequate, indeed, but the only report we have, and therefore priceless, by men, some more able and clear, others less able and clear, but *all* full of the influences of their time and condition, partakers of some of its simple or its learned ignorance— inevitably, in fine, expecting miracles and demanding them —a report, I say, by these men of that immense reality not fully or half fully grasped by them, *the mind of Christ—* then we shall be drawn to the Gospels with a new zest and as by a fresh spell. We shall throw ourselves upon their narratives with an ardour answering to the value of the pearl of great price they hold, and to the difficulty of reaching it.

So, to profit fully by the New Testament, the first thing to be done is to make it perfectly clear to oneself that its reporters both could err and did err. . . . Such a case we find in the confident expectation and assertion, on the part of the New Testament writers, of the approaching end of the world. Even this mistake people try to explain away; but it is so palpable that no words can cloud our perception of it. *The time is short. The Lord is at hand. The end of all things is at hand. Little children, it is the final time. The Lord's coming is at hand; behold, the judge standeth before the door.*[6] Nothing can really obscure the evidence furnished by such sayings as these. When Paul told the Thessalonians that they and he, at the approaching coming of Christ, should have their turn after, not before, the faithful dead—"For the Lord himself shall descend from heaven with a shout, with the voice of the archangel and with the trump of God, and the dead in Christ shall rise first, then we which are alive and remain shall be caught up together with them in the clouds, to meet the Lord in the air"[7]—when he said this, St. Paul was in truth simply mistaken in his notion of what was going to happen. This is as clear as anything can be. . . .

The miracles related in the Gospels will appear to us more and more, the more our experience and knowledge increases, to have but the same ground which is common to all miracles, the ground indicated by Shakespeare; to have been generated under the same kind of conditions as other miracles, and to follow the same laws. When once the "Zeit-Geist" has made us entertain the notion of this, a thousand things in the manner of relating will strike us which never struck us before, and will make us wonder how we could ever have thought differently. Discrepancies which we now labour with such honest pains and by such astonishing methods to explain away—the voice at Paul's conversion, heard by the bystanders according to one account, not heard by them according to another; the Holy Dove at Christ's baptism, visible to John the Baptist in one narrative, in two others to Jesus himself, in another, finally, to all the people

[6] I Corinthians 7:29; Philippians 4:5; I Peter 4:7; I John 2:18; James 5:8–9. We have here the express declarations of St. Paul, St. Peter, St. John and St. James.
[7] I Thessalonians 4:16, 17.

as well; the single blind man in one relation, growing into two blind men in another; the speaking with tongues, according to St. Paul a sound without meaning, according to the Acts an intelligent and intelligible utterance—all this will be felt to require really no explanation at all, to explain itself, to be natural to the whole class of incidents to which these miracles belong, and the inevitable result of the looseness with which the stories of them arise and are propagated.

And the more the miraculousness of the story deepens, as after the death of Jesus, the more does the texture of the incidents become loose and floating, the more does the very air and aspect of things seem to tell us we are in wonderland. Jesus after his resurrection not known by Mary Magdalene, taken by her for the gardener; appearing *in another form*, and not known by the two disciples going with him to Emmaus and at supper with him there; not known by his most intimate apostles on the borders of the Sea of Galilee—and presently, out of these vague beginnings, the recognitions getting asserted, then the ocular demonstrations, the final commissions, the ascension—one hardly knows which of the two to call the most evident here, the perfect simplicity and good faith of the narrators or the plainness with which they themselves really say to us: *Behold a legend growing under your eyes!*

And suggestions of this sort, with respect to the whole miraculous side of the New Testament, will meet us at every turn. It is neither our wish nor our design to accumulate them, to marshal them, to insist upon them, to make their force felt. Let those who desire to keep them at arm's length continue to do so, if they can, and go on placing the sanction of the Christian religion in its miracles. Our point is, that the objections to miracles do, and more and more will, without insistence, without attack, without controversy, make their own force felt; and that the sanction of Christianity, if Christianity is not to be lost along with its miracles, must be found elsewhere.

Chapter VI

The New Testament Record

1

Now, then, will be perceived the bearing and gravity of what I some little way back said, that the more we convince ourselves of the liability of the New Testament writers to mistake, the more we really bring out the greatness and worth of the New Testament. For the more the reporters were fallible and prone to delusion, the more does Jesus become independent of the mistakes they made, and unaffected by them. We have plain proof that here was a very great spirit; and the greater he was, the more certain were his disciples to misunderstand him. The depth of their misunderstanding of him is really a kind of measure of the height of his superiority. And this superiority is what interests us in the records of the New Testament; for the New Testament exists to reveal Jesus Christ, not to establish the immunity of its writers from error.

Jesus not to be confused with his reporters

Jesus himself is not a New Testament writer; he is the object of description and comment to the New Testament writers. As the Old Testament speaks about the Eternal and bears an invaluable witness to him, without yet ever adequately in words defining and expressing him; so, and even yet more, do the New Testament writers speak about Jesus and give a priceless record of him, without adequately and accurately comprehending him. They are altogether on another plane from Jesus, and their mistakes are not his. It is not Jesus himself who relates his own miracles to us; who tells us of his own apparitions after his death; who alleges

91

his crucifixion and sufferings as a fulfillment of the prophecy—*The Eternal keepeth all the bones of the righteous, so
that not one of them is broken*;[1] who proves salvation to be
by Christ alone, from the promise to Abraham being made
to *seed* in the singular number, not the plural. . . . [Jesus]
is reported to deal in miracles, to be above all a thaumaturgist. But the more his reporters were intellectually men of
their nation and time, and of its current beliefs—the more,
that is, they were open to mistakes—the more certain they
were to impute miracles to a wonderful and half-understood
personage like Jesus, whether he would or no. He himself
may, at the same time, have had quite other notions as to
what he was doing and intending.

Again, the mistake of imagining that the world was to
end, as St. Paul announces, within the lifetime of the first
Christian generation, is palpable. But the reporters of Jesus
make him announcing just the same thing: "This generation shall not pass away till they shall see the Son of Man
coming in the clouds with great power and glory, and then
shall he send his angels and gather his elect from the four
winds." [2] Popular theology can put a plain satisfactory
sense upon this, but, as usual, through that process described by Butler by which anything can be made to mean
anything; and from this sort of process the human mind is
beginning to shrink. A more plausible theology will say that
the words are an accommodation; that the speaker lends
himself to the fancies and expectations of his hearers. A
good deal of such accommodation there is in this and other
sayings of Jesus; but accommodation to the *full extent* here
supposed would surely have been impossible. To suppose it,
is most violent and unsatisfactory. Either, then, the words
were, like St. Paul's announcement, a mistake, or they are
not really the very words Jesus said, just as he said them.
That is, the reporters have given them a turn, however
slight, a tone and a colour, a connexion, to make them com-

[1] Psalms 34:20.   [2] Matthew 24:30–31, 34.

ply with a fixed idea in their own minds, which they unfeignedly believed was a fixed idea with Jesus also. Now, the more we regard the reporters of Jesus as men liable to err, full of the turbid Jewish fancies about "the grand consummation" which were then current, the easier we can understand these men inevitably putting their own eschatology into the mouth of Jesus, when they had to report his discourse about the kingdom of God and the troubles in store for the Jewish nation, and the less need have we to make Jesus a co-partner in their eschatology. . . .

In short, the more we conceive Jesus as almost as much over the heads of his disciples and reporters then, as he is over the heads of the mass of so-called Christians now, and the more we see his disciples to have been, as they were, men raised by a truer moral susceptiveness above their countrymen, but in intellectual conceptions and habits much on a par with them, all the more do we make room, so to speak, for Jesus to be a personage immensely great and wonderful; as wonderful as anything his reporters imagined him to be, though in a different manner.

2

Jesus rejected proof of miracle

We make room for him to be this, and through the inadequate reporting of his followers there breaks and shines, and will more and more break and shine the more the matter is examined, abundant evidence that he *was* this. It is most remarkable, and the best proof of the simplicity, seriousness, and good faith, which intercourse with Jesus Christ inspired, that witnesses with a fixed prepossession, and having no doubt at all as to the interpretation to be put on his acts and career, should yet admit so much of what makes against themselves and their own power of interpreting. For them, it was a thing beyond all doubt, that by miracles Jesus manifested forth his glory, and induced the faithful to believe in him. Yet what checks to this paramount and all-governing belief of theirs do they report from Jesus himself! Everybody will be able to recall such checks, although he may never yet have been accustomed to consider their full significance. *Except ye see signs and wonders, ye will not believe!* [3]—as much as to say: "Believe on right grounds you cannot, and you must needs believe on wrong!" And again: "Believe me that I am in the Father and the Father in me; *or else believe for the very works' sake!*" [4]—as much as to say: "Acknowledge me on the ground of my healing and restoring acts being miraculous, if you must; but it is not the right ground." No, not the right ground; and when Nicodemus came and would put conversion on this ground ("We know that thou art a teacher come from God, *for no one can do the miracles that thou doest except God be with him*"), Jesus rejoined: "Verily, verily, I say unto thee, *except a man be born from above,* he cannot see the kingdom of God!" thus tacitly changing his disciple's ground and correcting him.[5] Even distress and impatience at this false ground being taken is visible sometimes: "Jesus *groaned in his spirit* and said, Why doth this generation ask for a sign? Verily I say unto you, there shall no sign be given to this generation!" [6] Who does not see what double and treble importance these checks from Jesus to the reliance on miracles gain, through their being reported by those who relied on miracles devoutly? Who does not see a clue they offer as to the real mind of Jesus? To convey at all to such hearers of him that there was any objection to miracles, his own sense of the objection must have been profound; and to get them, who neither shared nor understood it, to repeat it a few times, he must have repeated it many times. . . .

---

3 John 4:48.   4 John 14:11.
5 John 3:2–3.   6 Mark 8:12.

Jesus's evidence internal—
the power that makes for righteousness

For the reporters of Jesus the rule was, undoubtedly, that men "believed on Jesus when they saw the miracles which he did." [7] Miracles were in these reporters' eyes, beyond question, the evidence of the Christian religion. And yet these same reporters indicate another and a totally different evidence offered for the Christian religion by Jesus Christ himself. *Every one that heareth and learneth from the Father, cometh unto me.*[8] *As the Father hath taught me, so I speak;*[9] *he that is of God heareth the words of God;*[10] *if God was your Father, ye would have loved me!* [11] This is inward evidence, direct evidence. From that previous knowledge of God, as "the Eternal that loveth righteousness," which Israel possessed, the hearers of Jesus could and should have concluded irresistibly, when they heard his words, that he came from God. Now, miracles are outward evidence, indirect evidence, not conclusive in this fashion. To walk on the sea cannot really prove a man to proceed from the Eternal that loveth righteousness; although undoubtedly, as we have said, a man who walks on the sea will be able to make the mass of mankind believe about him almost anything he chooses to say. But there is, after all, no necessary connexion between walking on the sea and proceeding from the Eternal that loveth righteousness. Jesus propounds, on the other hand, an evidence of which the whole force lies in the necessary connexion between the proving matter and the power that makes for righteousness. This is *his* evidence for the Christian religion.

His disciples felt the force of the evidence, indeed. Peter's answer to the question, "Will ye also go away?"— *"To whom should we go? thou hast the words of eternal*

[7] John 2:23.   [8] John 6:45.
[9] John 8:28.   [10] John 8:47.
[11] John 8:42.

life!" [12] proves it. But feeling the force of a thing is very different from understanding and possessing it. The evidence, which the disciples were *conscious* of understanding and possessing, was the evidence from miracles. And yet, in their report, Jesus is plainly shown to us insisting on a different evidence, an internal one. The character of the reporters gives to this indication a paramount importance. That they should indicate this internal evidence once, as the evidence on which Jesus insisted, is more significant, we say, than their indicating, twenty times, the evidence from miracles as the evidence naturally convincing to mankind, and recommended, as they thought, by Jesus. The notion of the one evidence they would have of themselves; the notion of the other they could only get from a superior mind. This mind must have been full of it to induce them to feel it at all; and their exhibition of it, even then, must of necessity be inadequate and broken.

But is it possible to overrate the value of the ground thus gained for showing the riches of the New Testament to those who, sick of the popular arguments from prophecy, sick of the popular arguments from miracles, are for casting the New Testament aside altogether? The book contains all that we know of a wonderful spirit, far above the heads of his reporters, still farther above the head of our popular theology, which has added its own misunderstanding of the reporters to the reporters' misunderstanding of Jesus. And it was quite inevitable that anything so superior and so profound should be imperfectly understood by those amongst whom it first appeared, and for a very long time afterwards; and that it should come at last gradually to stand out clearer only by time—*Time*, as the Greek maxim says, *the wisest of all things, for he is the unfailing discoverer.*

Yet, however much is discovered, the object of our scrutiny must still be beyond us, must still transcend our adequate knowledge, if for no other reason, because of the

[12] John 6:68.

character of the first and only records of him. But in the view now taken we have—even at the point to which we have already come—at least a wonderful figure transcending his time, transcending his disciples, attaching them but transcending them; in very much that he uttered going far above their heads, treating Scripture and prophecy like a master while they treated it like children, resting his doctrine on internal evidence while they rested it on miracles; and yet, by his incomparable lucidity and penetrativeness, planting his profound veins of thought in their memory along with their own notions and prepossessions, to come out all mixed up together, but still distinguishable one day and separable—and leaving his word thus to bear fruit for the future.

3

*Criticism must extract the saving doctrine
of Jesus from the Gospels*

Truly, then, some one will exclaim, we may say with the "Imitation": *Magna ars est scire conversari cum Jesu!* And so it is. To extract from his reporters the true Jesus entire, is even impossible; to extract him in considerable part is one of the highest conceivable tasks of criticism. And it is vain to use that favourite argument of popular theology that man could never have been left by Providence in difficulty and obscurity about a matter of so much importance to him. For the cardinal rule of our present inquiry is that rule of Newton's: *Hypotheses non fingo*; and this argument of popular theology rests on the eternal hypothesis of a magnified and non-natural man at the head of mankind's and the world's affairs. And a further answer is, that, as to the argument itself, even if we allowed the hypothesis, yet the course of things, so far as we can see, is *not* so; things, do *not* proceed in this fashion. Because a man has frequently to make sea-passages, he is *not* gifted with an immunity from

unchanging ground, on which the operations of Jesus both began and always proceeded.

And it is to be observed that Jesus by no means gave a new, more precise, scientific definition of God, but took up this term just as Israel used it, to stand for *the Eternal that loveth righteousness.* If therefore this term was, in Israel's use of it, not a term of science, but, as we say, a term of common speech, of poetry and eloquence, *thrown out* at a vast object of consciousness not fully covered by it, so it was in Jesus Christ's use of it also. And if the substratum of real affirmation in the term was, with Israel, not the affirmation of "a great Personal First Cause, the moral and intelligent Governor of the universe," but the affirmation of "an enduring Power, not ourselves, that makes for righteousness," so it remained with Jesus Christ likewise. He set going a great process of searching and sifting; but this process had for its direct object the idea of *righteousness,* and only touched the idea of God through this, and not independently of this and immediately. If the idea of righteousness was changed, this implied, undoubtedly, a corresponding change in the idea of the Power that makes for righteousness; but in this manner only, and to this extent, does the teaching of Jesus re-define the idea of God.

The method of Jesus

But search and sift and renew the idea of righteousness Jesus did. And though the work of Jesus, like the name of God, calls up in the believer a multitude of emotions and associations far more than any brief definition can cover, yet, remembering Jeremy Taylor's advice to avoid exhortations *to get Christ, to be in Christ,* and to seek some more distinct and practical way of speaking of him, we shall not do ill, perhaps, if we summarise to our own minds his work by saying, that he restored the intuition of God through transforming the idea of righteousness; and that, to do this, he brought a *method,* and he brought a *secret.* And of those two great words which fill such a place in his gospel, *repent-*

ance and *peace*—as we see that his Apostles, when they preached his gospel, preached *"Repentance* unto life" [3] and *"Peace* through Jesus Christ," [4]—of these two great words, one, *repentance,* attaches itself, we shall find, to his *method,* and the other, *peace,* to his *secret.*

There was no question between Jesus Christ and the Jews as to the object to aim at. "If thou wouldst enter into life, keep the commandments," said Jesus.[5] And Israel, too, on his part, said: "He that keepeth the commandments keepeth his own soul." [6] But *what* commandments? The commandments of God; about this, too, there was no question. But: "Leaving the commandment of God, ye hold the *tradition of men;* ye make the commandment of God of none effect by your *tradition";* said Jesus.[7] Therefore the commandments which Israel followed were *not* commandments of God by which a man keeps his own soul, enters into life. And the practical proof of this was, that Israel stood before the eyes of the world manifestly neither blessed nor at peace; yet these characters of bliss and peace the following of the real commandments of God was confessed to give. So a rule, or method, was wanted, by which to determine on what the keeping of the real commandments of God depended.

And Jesus gave one: "The things that come from *within a man's heart,* they it is which defile him!" [8]

We have seen what an immense matter conduct is— that it is three-fourths of life. We have seen how plain and simple a matter it is, so far as knowledge is concerned. We have seen how, moreover, philosophers are for referring all conduct to one or other of man's two elementary instincts— the instinct of self-preservation and the reproductive instinct. It is the suggestions of one or other of these instincts, philosophers say, which call forth all cases in which there is

---

[3] Acts 11:18.
[5] Matthew 19:17.
[7] Mark 7:9, 13.

[4] Acts 10:36.
[6] Proverbs 19:16.
[8] Matthew 15:18; Mark 7:20–21.

scope for exercising morality, or conduct. And this does, we saw, cover the facts well enough. For we can run up nearly all faults of conduct into two classes—faults of temper and faults of sensuality; to be referred, all of them, to one or other of these two instincts. Now, Jesus not only says that things coming from within a man's heart defile him, he adds expressly what these things that, coming from within a man, defile him, are. And what he enumerates are the following: "Evil thoughts, adulteries, fornications, murders, stealings, greeds, viciousnesses, fraud, dissoluteness, envy, evil-speaking, pride, folly." [9] These fall into two groups: one, of faults of self-assertion, graspingness and violence, all of which we may call faults of *temper*; and the other, of faults of *sensuality*. And the two groups, between them, do for practical purposes cover all the range of faults proceeding from these two sources, and therefore all the range of conduct. So the motions or impulses to faults of *conduct* were what Jesus said the real commandments of God are concerned with. And it was plain what such faults are; but, to make assurance more sure, he went farther and said what they are. But no outward observances were *conduct*, were that keeping of the commandments of God which was the keeping of a man's own soul and made him enter into life. To have the *heart* and *thoughts* in order as to certain matters, was conduct.

This was the "method" of Jesus: the setting up a great unceasing inward movement of attention and verification in matters which are three-fourths of human life, where to see true and to verify is not difficult, the difficult thing is to care and to attend. And the inducement to attend was because joy and peace, missed on every other line, were to be reached on this.

[9] Mark 7:21, 22.

2

The secret of Jesus

But for this world of busy inward movement created by the *method* of Jesus, a rule of action was wanted; and this rule was found in his *secret*. It was this of which the Apostle Paul afterwards possessed himself with such energy, and called it "the word of the cross," [10] or, *necrosis*, "dying." The rule of action St. Paul gave was: "Always bearing about in the body the *dying* of Jesus, that the *life* also of Jesus may be made manifest in our body!" [11] In the popular theurgy, these words are commonly referred to what is called "pleading the blood of the covenant"—relying on the death and merits of Christ (in pursuance of the contract originally passed in the Council of the Trinity) to satisfy God's wrath against sinners and to redeem us. But they do really refer to words of Jesus, often and often repeated, and of which the following may very well stand as pre-eminently representative: *"He that will save his life shall lose it; he that will lose his life shall save it. He that loveth his life shall lose it, and he that hateth his life in this world shall keep it unto life eternal. Whosoever will come after me, let him renounce himself, and take up his cross daily, and follow me."* [12]

These words, or words like them, were repeated again and again, so that no reporter could miss them. No reporter did miss them. We find them, as we find the *method* of conscience, in all the four Gospels. Perhaps there is no other maxim of Jesus which has such a combined stress of evidence for it, and may be taken as so eminently his. And no wonder. For the maxim contains his secret, the secret by which, emphatically, his gospel "brought life and immortality to light." [13] Christ's *method* directed the disciple's eye inward, and set his consciousness to work; and the first thing

[10] I Corinthians 1:18.   [11] II Corinthians 4:10.
[12] Luke 9:24; John 12:25; Luke 9:23.
[13] II Timothy 1:10.

his consciousness told him was, that he had two selves pulling him different ways. Till we attend, till the *method* is set at work, it seems as if "the wishes of the flesh and of the current thoughts" [14] were to be followed as a matter of course; as if an impulse to do a thing must mean that we should do it. But when we attend, we find that an impulse to do a thing is really in itself no reason at all why we should do it; because impulses proceed from two sources, quite different, and of quite different degrees of authority. St. Paul contrasts them as the inward man, and the man in our members; the mind of the flesh, and the spiritual mind.[15] Jesus contrasts them as *life,* properly so named, and *life in this world*.[16] And the moment we seriously attend to conscience, to the suggestions which concern practice and conduct, we can see plainly enough from which source a suggestion comes, and that the suggestions from one source are to overrule those from the other.

But this is a negative state of things, a reign of check and constraint, a reign, merely, of morality. Jesus changed it into what was positive and attractive, lighted it up, made it religion, by the idea of *two lives*. One of them *life* properly so called, full of light, endurance, felicity, in connexion with the higher and permanent self; and the other of them life improperly so called, in connexion with the lower and transient self. The first kind of life was already a cherished ideal with Israel ("Thou wilt show me the path of life!";[17] and a man might be placed in it, Jesus said, by dying to the second. For it is to be noted that our common expression, "*deny* himself," is an inadequate and misleading version of the words used by Jesus. To deny one's self is commonly understood to mean that one refuses one's self something. But what Jesus says is: "Let a man *disown* himself, *renounce* himself, die as regards his old self, and so live." *Himself,* the *old man,* the *life in this world,* meant follow-

[14] Ephesians 2:3.
[16] John 12:25.

[15] Romans 8.
[17] Psalms 16:11.

ing those "wishes of the flesh and of the current thoughts" which Jesus had, by his method, already put his disciples in the way of sifting and scrutinising, and of trying by the standard of conformity to conscience.

Thus, after putting him by his method in the way to find *what* doing righteousness was, by his secret Jesus put the disciple in the way of *doing* it. For the breaking the sway of what is commonly called *one's self*, ceasing our concern with it and leaving it to perish, is not, Jesus said, being thwarted or crossed, but *living*. And the proof of this is that it has the characters of life in the highest degree—the sense of going right, hitting the mark, succeeding. That is, it has the characters of *happiness*; and happiness is, for Israel, the same thing as having the Eternal with us, seeing the salvation of God. "The tree," as Jesus said, and as men's common sense and proverbial speech say with him, "is known by its *fruits*"; [18] and Jesus, then, was to be received by Israel as sent from God, because the secret of Jesus leads to the salvation of God, which is what Israel most desired. *The word of the cross*, in short, turned out to be at the same time *the word of the kingdom*.[19] And to this experimental sanction of his secret, this sense it gives of having the Eternal on our side and approving us, Jesus appealed when he said of himself: *"Therefore* doth my Father love me, because I lay down my life, that I may take it again."* [20] This, again, in our popular theurgy, is materialised into the First Person of the Trinity approving the Second, because he stands to the contract already in the Council of the Trinity passed. But what it really means is, that the joy of Jesus, of this "Son of Peace," [21] the "joy" he was so desirous that his disciples should find "fulfilled in themselves," [22] was due to his having himself followed his own secret. And the great counterpart to: *A life-giving change of the inner man*—the promise:

[18] Matthew 12:33.
[19] Matthew 13:19.
[20] John 10:17.
[21] Luke 10:6.
[22] John 17:13.

Peace through Jesus Christ! [23]—is peace through this secret
of his.

Jesus's secret confirmed in experience

Now, the value of this rule that one should die to one's
apparent self, live to one's real self, depends upon whether
it is true. And true it certainly is—a profound truth of what
our scientific friends, who have a systematic philosophy and
a nomenclature to match, and who talk of *Egoism* and *Al-
truism*, would call, perhaps, psycho-physiology. And we may
trace men's experience affirming and confirming it, from a
very plain and level account of it to an account almost as
high and solemn as that of Jesus. That an opposition there
is, in all matter of what we call *conduct,* between a man's
first impulses and what he ultimately finds to be the real law
of his being; that a man accomplishes his right function as a
man, fulfils his end, hits the mark, in giving effect to the real
law of his being; and that happiness attends his thus hitting
the mark—all good observers report. No statement of this
general experience can be simpler or more faithful than one
given us by that great naturalist, Aristotle.[24] "In all wholes
made up of parts," says he, "there is a ruler and a ruled;
throughout nature this is so; we see it even in things without life, they have their *harmony* or *law.* The living being is
composed of soul and body, whereof the one is naturally
ruler and the other ruled. Now what is natural we are to
learn from what fulfils the law of its nature most, and not
from what is depraved. So we ought to take the man who
has the best disposition of body and soul; and in him we
shall find that this is so; for in people that are grievous both
to others and to themselves the body may often appear ruling the soul, because such people are poor creatures and
false to nature." And Aristotle goes on to distinguish between the *body,* over which, he says, the rule of the soul is
absolute, and the *movement of thought and desire,* over

[23] Acts 11:18; 10:36.   [24] *Politics* i. 5.

which reason has, says he, "a constitutional rule," in words which exactly recall St. Paul's phrase for our double enemy: "the *flesh* and the *current thoughts*." So entirely are we here on ground of general experience. And if we go on and take this maxim from Stobaeus: "All fine acquirement implies a foregoing *effort* of *self-control*; or this from Horace: "*Rule* your current self or it will rule *you*! bridle it in and chain it down!" or this from Goethe's autobiography: "Everything cries out to us that we must *renounce*"; or still more this from his *Faust*: "Thou must *go without, go without!* that is the everlasting song which every hour, all our life through, hoarsely sings to us!—then we have testimony not only to the necessity of this natural law of rule and suppression, but also to the strain and labour and suffering which attend it. But when we come a little further and take a sentence like this of Plato: "Of sufferings and pains cometh *help*, for it is not possible by any other way to be ridded of our iniquity," then we get a higher strain, a strain like St. Peter's: "He that hath suffered in the flesh hath ceased from sin";[25] and we are brought to see, not only the *necessity* of the law of rule and suppression, not only the *pain* and *suffering* in it, but also its beneficence. And this positive sense of beneficence, salutariness, and hope, comes out yet more strongly when Wordsworth says to Duty: "Nor know we anything so fair as is the smile upon thy face"; or when Bishop Wilson says: "They that deny themselves will be sure to find their strength increased, their affections raised, and their inward peace continually augmented"; and most of all, perhaps, when we hear from Goethe: "Die and come to life! for so long as this is not accomplished thou art but a troubled guest upon an earth of gloom!" But this is evidently borrowed from Jesus, and by one whose testimony is of all the more weight, because he certainly would not have become thus a borrower from Jesus, unless the truth had compelled him.

[25] I Peter 4:1.

Self-denial brings joy and life

And never certainly was the joy, which in self-renounce-ment underlies the pain, so brought out as when Jesus boldly called the suppression of our first impulses and cur-rent thoughts: *life, real life, eternal life.* So that Jesus not only *saw* this great necessary truth of there being, as Aris-totle says, in human nature a part to rule and a part to be ruled; he saw it so *thoroughly,* that he saw through the suffering at its surface to the joy at its centre, filled it with promise and hope, and made it infinitely attractive. As Israel, therefore, is "the people of righteousness," because, though others have perceived the importance of righteous-ness, Israel, above everyone, perceived the *happiness* of it; so self-renouncement, the main factor in conduct or right-eousness, is "the secret of Jesus," because, although others have seen that it was necessary, Jesus, above everyone, saw that it was *peace, joy, life. . . .*

This, we say, is of the very essence of his secret of self-renouncement, as of his method of inwardness—that its truth will be found to commend itself by *happiness,* to prove itself by *happiness.* And of the secret more especially is this true. And as we have said, that though there gathers round the word "God" very much besides, yet we shall in general, in reading the Bible, get the surest hold on the word "God" by giving it the sense of *the Eternal Power, not ourselves, which makes for righteousness,* so we shall get the best hold on many expressions of Jesus by referring them, though they include more, yet primarily and pointedly to his "secret" and to the happiness which this contained. *Bread of life, living water,* these are, in general, Jesus, Jesus in his whole being and in his total effect; but in especial they are Jesus as offering his *secret.* And when Jesus says: "He that eateth me shall live by me!" [26] we shall under-stand the words best if we think of his *secret.*

[26] John 6:57.

And so again with the famous words to the woman by the well in Samaria: "Whosoever drinketh of *this* water shall thirst again, but whosoever drinketh of the water that I shall give him shall never thirst, but the water that I shall give him shall be in him a spring of water welling up unto everlasting life." [27] These words, how are we are to take them, so as to reach their meaning best? What distinctly *is* this "water that I shall give him"? Jesus himself and his word, no doubt; yet so we come but to that very notion, which Jeremy Taylor warns us against as vague, of *getting Christ.* The Bishop of Gloucester will tell us, perhaps, that it is "the blessed truth that the Creator of the universe is a Person," or the doctrine of the consubstantiality of the Eternal Son. But surely it would be a strong figure of speech to say of these doctrines, that a man, after receiving them, could never again feel thirsty! See, on the contrary, how the words suit *the secret*: "He that loveth his life shall lose it, and he that hateth his life in this world shall keep it unto life eternal." This "secret of Jesus," as we call it, will be found applicable to all the thousand problems which the exercise of conduct daily offers; it alone can solve them all happily, and may indeed be called "a spring of water welling up unto everlasting life." And, in general, wherever the words *life* and *death* are used by Jesus, we shall do well to have his "secret" at hand; for in his thoughts, on these occasions, it is never far off.

And now, too, we can see why it is a mistake, and may lead to much error, to exhibit any series of maxims, like those of the Sermon on the Mount, as the ultimate sum and formula into which Christianity may run up. Maxims of this kind are but *applications* of the method and the secret of Jesus; and the method and secret are capable of yet an infinite number more of such applications. Christianity is a *source*; no one supply of water and refreshment that comes from it can be called the sum of Christianity.

[27] John 4:13–14.

3

Jesus's sweet reasonableness

A method of *inwardness,* a secret of self-renouncement
—but can any statement of what Jesus brought be complete,
which does not include that temper of *mildness* and *sweetness* in which both of these worked? To the representative
texts already given there is certainly to be added this other:
*"Learn of me that I am mild and lowly in heart, and ye
shall find rest unto your souls!"* [28] Shall we attach mildness
to the *method,* because, without it, a clear and limpid view
inwards is impossible? Or shall we attach it to the *secret?*—
the dying to faults of temper is a part, certainly, of dying to
one's ordinary self, one's *life in this world. Mildness,* however, is rather an element in which, in Jesus, both method
and secret worked; the medium through which both the
method and secret were exhibited. We may think of it as
perfectly illustrated and exemplified in his answer to the
foolish question, *Who is the greatest in the kingdom of
heaven?*—when, taking a little child and setting him in the
midst, he said: "Whosoever receives the kingdom of God as
a little child, the same is the greatest in it." [29] Here are
both inward appraisal and self-renouncement; but what is
most admirable is the sweet reasonableness, the exquisite,
mild, winning felicity, with which the renouncement and
the inward appraisal are applied and conveyed. And the
conjunction of the three in Jesus—the method of inwardness, and the secret of self-renouncement working in and
through this element of mildness—produced the total impression of his "epieikeia," * or sweet reasonableness; a
total impression ineffable and indescribable for the disciples, as also it was irresistible for them, but at which their

[28] Matthew 11:29.   [29] Matthew 18:1–4; Mark 10:15.
    * The R. S. V. translates *epieikeia* as "gentleness."—*Ed.*

descriptive words, words like this *"sweet reasonableness,"* and *"full of grace and truth,"* are thrown out and aimed.[30]

And this total stamp of "grace and truth," this exquisite conjunction and balance, in an element of mildness, of a method of inwardness perfectly handled and a self-renouncement perfectly kept, was found in Jesus alone. What are the method of inwardness and the secret of self-renouncement without the sure balance of Jesus, without his *epieikeia?* Much, but very far indeed from what he showed or what he meant; they come to be used blindly, used mechanically, used amiss, and lead to the strangest aberrations. St. Simeon Stylites on his column, Pascal girdled with spikes, Lacordaire flogging himself on his deathbed, are what the *secret* by itself produces. The *method* by itself gives us our political Dissenter, pluming himself on some irrational "conscientious objections," and not knowing, that with conscience he has done nothing until he has got to the bottom of conscience, and made it tell him *right.* Therefore the disciples of Jesus were not told to believe in his method, or to believe in his secret, but to believe in *him*; they were not told to follow the method or to follow the secret, but they were told: "Follow *me!*" For it was only by fixing their heart and mind on Jesus that they could learn to use the method and secret right; by "feeding on him," by, as he often said, *"remaining* in him."

But this is just what Israel had been told to do as regards the Eternal himself. "I have set the Eternal *always before me"*; "Mine eyes are *ever toward* the Eternal"; "The Eternal is the *strength of my life"*; *"Wait,* I say, *on* the Eternal!" [31] Now, then, let us go back again for a little to Israel, and to Israel's belief.

---

[30] Bossuet calls him *le débonnaire Jésus;* Cowper speaks of his questioning the disciples going to Emmaus "with a *kind, engaging* air."   [31] Psalms 16:8; 25:15; 27:1, 14.

Chapter VIII

Faith in Christ

1

As the Jews were always talking about the Messiah, so they were always talking, we know, about God. And they believed in God's Messiah after their notion of him, because they believed in God after their notion of *him*—but both notions were wrong. All their aspirations were now turned towards the Messiah; whoever would do them good, must first change their ideal of the Messiah. But their ideal of God's Messiah depended upon their notion of God. This notion was now false, like their ideal of the Messiah; but once it had been true, or, at least, true comparatively—once Israel had had the intuition of God as *the Eternal that loveth righteousness*. And the intuition had never been so lost but that it was capable of being revived. To change their dangerous and misleading ideal of God's Messiah, therefore, and to make the Jews believe in the true Messiah, could only be accomplished by bringing them back to a truer notion of God and his righteousness. By this it could, perhaps, be accomplished, but by this only.

Jesus avoids all theological speculation

And this is what Jesus sought to do. He sought to do it in the way we have seen, by his "method" and his "secret." First, by his "method" of a change of the inner man. "Do not be all abroad, *do not be in the air*,"[1] he said to his nation. "You look for the kingdom of God. The kingdom of God is the reign of righteousness, God's will done by all mankind. Well, then, seek the kingdom of God! *the king-*

[1] Luke 12:29.

dom of God is within you!" [2] And, next, by his "secret" of peace. *"Renounce thyself, and take up thy cross daily and follow me!* [3] *He that loveth his life shall lose it, and he that hateth his life in this world shall keep it unto life eternal."* [4] And the revolution thus made was so immense, that the least in this new kingdom of heaven, this realm of the "method" and the "secret," was greater, Jesus said, than one who, like John the Baptist, was even greatest in the old realm of Jewish religion.[5] And those who obeyed the gospel of this new kingdom came to the *light;* [6] they had *joy;* [7] they entered into *peace;* [8] they ceased to *thirst:* the word became in them a spring of water welling up unto *everlasting life.*[9] But these were the admitted tests of righteousness, of obeying the voice of the Eternal who loveth righteousness. "There ariseth *light* for the righteous, and *gladness* for the upright in heart; [10] he that feareth the Eternal, *blessed* is he!" [11]

Now, the special value of the Fourth Gospel is, not that it exhibits the method and secret of Jesus—for all the Gospels exhibit them—but that it exhibits the establishment of them by means of Israel's own idea of God, cleared and re-awakened. The argument is: "Your are always talking about God, God's word, righteousness; always saying that God is your Father, and will send his Messiah for your salvation. Well, he who receives me shows that he talks about God with a knowledge of what he is saying; he *sets to his seal* that God is true.[12] *He who is of God heareth the words of God;*[13] *every one that heareth and learneth of the Father cometh unto me,*[14] *and ye have not his word abiding in you, because whom he hath sent, him ye believe not;*[15] *if any one will do God's will he shall know of the doctrine,*

[2] Luke 17:21.
[3] Luke 9:23.
[4] John 12:25.
[5] Matthew 11:11.
[6] John 3:21.
[7] John 17:13.
[8] John 16:33.
[9] John 4:14.
[10] Psalms 97:11.
[11] Psalms 112:1.
[12] John 3:33.
[13] John 8:47.
[14] John 6:45.
[15] John 5:38.

whether it be of God." [16] This, therefore, is what Jesus said
—"I, whose message of salvation is: *if a man keep my word
he shall never see death!* [17] am sent of God; because he, who
obeys my saying: *Renounce thyself and follow me!* [18] shall
feel that he truly lives, and that he is following, therefore,
Israel's God of whom it is said: *Thou wilt show me the path
of life."* [19]

The doctrine therefore is double—*Renounce thyself,*
the secret of Jesus, involving a foregoing exercise of his
method; and, *Follow me, who am sent from God!* That is
the favourite expression—*Sent from God.* "I come forth
from the Father; the Father hath sent me; God hath sent
me." [20] Now this identified Jesus and his salvation with the
Messiah whom, with his salvation, the Jews were expecting.
For his disciples therefore, and for Christendom after them,
Jesus was and is the *Messiah* or *Christ.*

Meanwhile, as with the word *God,* so with the word
Christ. Jesus did not give any scientific definition of it—
such as, for instance, that Christ was the Logos. He took the
word Christ as the Jews used it, as he took the word *God* as
the Jews used it. And as he amended their notion of God,
the Eternal who loveth righteousness, by showing what
righteousness really was, so he amended their notion of the
Messiah, the *chosen bringer of God's salvation,* by showing
what *salvation* really was. And though his own application
of terms to designate himself is not a matter where we can
perfectly trust his reporters (as it is clear, for instance, that
the writer of the Fourth Gospel was more metaphysical than
Jesus himself) ,[21] yet there is no difficulty in supposing him

[16] John 7:17.   [17] John 8:51.
[18] Matthew 16:24.   [19] Psalms 16:11.
[20] John 16:27, 28, 30; 6:57; 7:29; 8:42; 17:8.
[21] It is to be remembered, too, that whereas Jesus spoke in
Aramaic, the most concrete and unmetaphysical of languages, he
is reported in Greek, the most metaphysical. What, in the mouth
of Jesus, was the word which comes to us as μονογενής (*only begotten)?* Probably the simple Aramaic word for *unique, only.* And

to have applied to himself each and all the terms which the Jews in any way used to describe the Messiah—*Messiah* or *Christ,* God's *Chosen* or *Beloved* or *Consecrated* or *Glorified One,* the *Son of God,* the *Son of Man;* because his concern, as we have said, was with his countrymen's idea of salvation, not with their terms for designating the bringer of it. But the simplest term, the term which gives least opening into theosophy—*Son of Man*—he certainly preferred. So, too, he loved the simple expressions "God *sent* me," "The Father *hath sent* me"; and he chose so often to say, in a general manner, "I am *He*," [22] rather than to say positively, "I am the *Christ*."

And evidently this mode of speaking struck his hearers. We find the Jews saying: "How long dost thou *make us to doubt*? if thou be the Christ, tell us *plainly*." [23] And even then Jesus does not answer point-blank, but prefers to say: "I have told you, and ye believe not." Yet this does not imply that he had the least doubt or hesitation in naming himself the Messiah, the Son of God; but only that his concern was, as we have said, with God's *righteousness* and Christ's *salvation,* and that he avoided all use of the names *God,* and *Christ,* which might give an opening into mere theosophical speculation. And this is shown, moreover, by the largeness and freedom—almost, one may say, indifference—of his treatment of both names; as names, in using which, his hearers were always in danger of going off into a theosophy that did them no good and had better occupy them as little as possible. *"I and my Father are one!"* [24] he would say at one time; and *"My Father is greater than I!"* [25] at another. When the Jews were offended at his calling himself the Son of God, he quotes Scripture to show that even mere men were in Scripture called *Gods*; and for you,

---

yet, in the Greek record, even the word μονογενής is not, like *only begotten* in our translation, reserved for Christ; see Luke vii. 12; viii. 42; ix. 38.

[22] John 4:26; 8:24, 28.   [23] John 10:24.
[24] John 10:30.   [25] John 14:28.

he says, who go by the letter of Scripture, surely this is sanction enough for calling anyone, whom God sends, *the Son of God!* [26] He did not at all mean, that the Messiah was a son of God merely in the sense in which any great man might be so called; but he meant that these questions of theosophy were useless for his hearers, and that they puzzled themselves with them in vain. All they were concerned with was, that *he* was the Messiah they expected, sent to them with salvation from God. . . .

2

Inevitable that Jesus's words be misconstrued

Thus, then, did Jesus seek to transform the immense materialising *Aberglaube,* into which the religion of Israel had fallen, and to spiritualise it at all points; while in his method and secret he supplied a sure basis for practice. But to follow him entirely there was needed an *epieikeia,* an unfailing sweetness and unerring perception, like his own. It was much if his disciples got firm hold on his method and his secret; and if they transmitted fragments enough of his lofty spiritualism to make it in the fullness of time discernible, and to make it at once and from the first in a large degree serviceable. Who can read in the Gospels the comments preserved to us, both of disciples and of others, on what he said, and not feel that Jesus must have known, while he nevertheless persevered in saying them, how things like: *"Before Abraham was, I am,"* [27] or: *"I will not leave you comfortless, I will come unto you,"* [28] would be misapprehended by those who heard them?

But, indeed, Jesus himself tells us that he knew and foresaw this. With the promise of the Spirit of truth which should, after his departure, work in his disciples first, then

[26] John 10:34–36.   [27] John 8:58.
[28] John 14:18.

in the world, and which should convince the world of sin, of righteousness, and of judgment, and finally transform it, we are all familiar. But we do not enough remark the impressive words, uttered to the crowd around him only a little while before, and of far wider application than the reporter imagined: *"Yet a little while is the light with you; walk while ye have the light, lest the darkness overtake you unawares!"* [29] The real application cannot have been to the unconverted only; a call to the unconverted to make haste because their chance of conversion would soon, with Christ's departure, be gone. No, converts came in far thicker after Christ's departure than in his life. The words are for the converted also. It is as if Jesus foresaw the want of his sweet reasonableness, which he could not leave, to help his method and his secret, which he could leave; as if he foresaw his words misconstrued, his rising to eternal life turned into a physical miracle, the advent of the Spirit of truth turned into a scene of thaumaturgy, Peter proving his Master's Messiahship from a Psalm that does not prove it, the great Apostle of the Gentiles word-splitting like a pedantic Rabbi, the most beautiful soul among his own reporters saddling him with metaphysics—foresaw the growth of creeds, the growth of dogma, and so through all the confusion worse confounded of councils, schoolmen, and confessions of faith, down to our own two bishops bent on "doing something" for the honour of the Godhead of the Eternal Son!

[29] John 12:35.

Chapter IX

Aberglaube Re-invading

1

Miracles, and, above all, the crowning miracles of the Resurrection and Ascension to be followed by the second Advent, were from the first firmly fixed as parts of the disciples' belief. *"Behold, he cometh with clouds: and every eye shall see him, and they also which pierced him, and all kindreds of the earth shall wail because of him!"* [1] As time went on, and Christianity spread wider and wider among the multitudes, and with less and less of control from the personal influence of Jesus, Christianity developed more and more its side of miracle and legend; until to believe Jesus to be the Son of God meant to believe the points of the legend—his preternatural conception and birth, his miracles, his descent into hell, his bodily resurrection, his ascent into heaven, and his future triumphant return to judgment. And these and like matters are what popular religion drew forth from the records of Jesus as the essentials of belief. These essentials got embodied in a short formulary; and so the creed which is called the Apostles' Creed came together.

Creeds—the popular and learned science of Christianity

It is not the apostles' creed, for it took more than five hundred years to grow to maturity. It was not the creed of any single doctor or body of doctors, but it was a sort of summary of Christianity which the people, the Church at large, would naturally develop; it is the *popular science* of

[1] Revelation 1:7.

Christianity. Given the alleged charge: "Go ye and teach all nations, baptising them in the name of the Father, the Son, and the Holy Spirit," [2] and the candidate for baptism would naturally come to have a profession of faith to make respecting that whereinto he was baptized; this profession of faith would naturally become just such a summary as the Apostles' Creed. It contains no mention of either the "method" or the "secret," it is occupied entirely with external facts; and it may be safely said, not only that such a summary of religious faith could never have been delivered by Jesus, but it could never have been adopted as adequate by any of his principal apostles, by Peter, or Paul, or John. But it is, as we have said, the *popular science* of Christianity.

Years proceeded. The world came in to Christianity; the world, and the world's educated people, and the educated people's Aryan genius with its turn for making religion a metaphysical conception; and all this in a time of declining criticism, a time when the possibility of true scientific criticism, in any direction whatever, was lessening rather than increasing. The popular science was found not elaborate enough to satisfy. Ingenious men took its terms and its data, and applied to them, not an historical criticism showing how they arose, but abstruse metaphysical conceptions. And so we have the so-called Nicene Creed, which is the *learned science* of Christianity, as the Apostles' Creed is the popular science.

Compare the words of St. Augustine
with those of the Bible

Now, how this learned science is related to the Bible we shall feel, if we compare the religious utterances of its doctors with the religious utterances of the Bible. Suppose, for instance, we compare with the Psalms the *Soliloquies* of St. Augustine, a truly great and religious man; and of St. Augustine, not in school and controversy, but in religious

[2] Matthew 28:19.

soliloquy. St. Augustine prays: "Come to my help, thou one God, one eternal true substance, where is no discrepancy, no confusion, no transience, no indigency, no death; where is supreme concord, supreme evidence, supreme constancy, supreme plenitude, supreme life; where nothing is lacking, nothing is over and above; where he who begets and he who is begotten of him are one; God, above whom is nothing, outside whom is nothing, without whom is nothing; God, beneath whom is the whole, in whom is the whole, with whom is the whole . . . hearken, hearken, hearken, unto me, my God, my Lord; open thy door unto me that knock!" And a further *Book of Soliloquies,* popularly ascribed to St. Augustine and printed with his works, but probably of a later date and author, shows the full-blown development of all this, shows the inevitable results of bringing to the idea of God this play of intellectual fancy so alien to the Bible. The passages we will quote take evidently their inspiration from the words of St. Augustine just given, and retain even in some degree his very forms of expression: "Holy Trinity, superadmirable Trinity, and superinerrable, and super-inscrutable, and superinaccessible, superincomprehensible, superintelligible, superessential, superessentially surpassing all sense, all reason, all intellect, all intelligence, all essence of supercelestial minds; which can neither be said, nor thought, nor understood, nor known even by the eyes of angels!" And again, more practically, but still in the same style: "O three co-equal and co-eternal Persons, one and true God, Father and Son and Holy Ghost, who by thyself inhabitest eternity and light inaccessible, who hast founded the earth in thy power, and rulest the world by thy prudence, Holy, Holy, Holy, Lord God of Sabaoth, terrible and strong, just and merciful, admirable, laudable, amiable, one God, three persons, one essence, power, wisdom, goodness, one and undivided Trinity, open unto me that cry unto Thee the gates of righteousness!"

And now compare this with the Bible—*Teach me to do the thing that pleaseth thee, for thou art my God! let thy*

loving spirit lead me forth into the land of righteousness! [3]
That is Israel's way of praying! that is how a poor ill-endowed Semite, belonging to the occipital races, unhelped by the Aryan genius and ignorant that religion is a metaphysical conception, talks religion! and we see what a different thing he makes of it.

But, finally, the original Semite fell more and more into the shade. The Aryans came to the front, the notion of religion being a metaphysical conception prevailed. But the doctors differed in their metaphysics; and the doctors who conquered enshrined their victorious form of metaphysics in a creed, the so-called Creed of St. Athanasius, which is learned science like the Nicene Creed, but learned science which has fought and got ruffled by fighting, and is fiercely dictatorial now that it has won; learned science *with a strong dash of violent and vindictive temper*. Thus we have the three creeds: the so-called Apostles' Creed, popular science; the Nicene Creed, learned science; the Athanasian Creed, learned science with a strong dash of temper. And the two latter are founded on the first, taking its data just as they stand, but dressing them metaphysically.

Now this first Creed is founded on a supposed final charge from Jesus to his apostles: "Go ye and teach all nations, baptizing them in the name of the Father, the Son, and the Holy Ghost!" [4] It explains and expands what Jesus here told his apostles to baptize the world into. But we have already remarked the difference in character between the narrative, in the Gospels, of what happened before Christ's death, and the narrative of what happened after it. For all words of Jesus placed *after* his death, the internal evidence becomes preeminently important. He may well have said words attributed to him, but not then. So the speech to Thomas, "Because thou hast seen me thou hast believed; blessed are they who have not seen and yet have believed!" [5]

[3] Psalms 143:10.   [4] Matthew 28:19.
[5] John 20:29.

may quite well have been a speech of Jesus uttered on some occasion during his life, and then transferred to the story of the days after his resurrection and made the centre of this incident of the doubt of Thomas. On the other hand, again, the prophecy of the details of Peter's death[6] is almost certainly an addition after the event, because it is not at all in the manner of Jesus. What *is* in his manner, and what he had probably at some time said, are the words given elsewhere: "Whither I go thou canst not follow me now, but thou shalt follow me afterwards." [7] So, too, it is extremely improbable that Jesus should have ever charged his apostles to "baptize all nations in the name of the Father, the Son, and the Holy Ghost." There is no improbability in his investing them with a very high commission. He may perfectly well have said: "Whosoever sins ye remit, they are remitted; whosoever sins ye retain, they are retained." [8] But it is almost impossible he can have given this charge to baptize in the name of the Father, the Son, and the Holy Ghost; it is by far too systematic and what people are fond of calling an *anachronism*. It is not the least like what Jesus was in the habit of saying, and it is just like what would be attributed to him as baptism and its formula grew in importance. The genuine charge of Jesus to his apostles was, almost certainly: "As my Father sent me, even so send I you," [9] and not this. So that our three creeds, and with them the whole of our so-called orthodox theology, are founded upon words which Jesus in all probability never uttered.

2

We may leave all questions about the Church, its rise, and its organization, out of sight altogether. Much as is made of them, they are comparatively unimportant. Jesus

---

[6] John 21:18.   [7] John 13:36.
[8] John 20:23.   [9] John 20:21.

never troubled himself with what are called Church matters at all; his attention was fixed solely upon the individual. His apostles did what was necessary, as such matters came to require a practical notice and arrangement; but to the apostles, too, they were still quite secondary. The Church grew into something quite different from what they or Jesus had, or could have had, any thought of. But this was of no importance in itself; and how believers should organise their society as circumstances changed, circumstances themselves might very well decide.

The one important question was and is, how believers laid and kept hold on the revelations contained in the Bible; because for the sake of these it confessedly is, that every church exists. Even the apostles, we have seen, did not lay hold on them perfectly. In their attachment to miracles, in the prominence they gave to the crowning miracles of Christ's bodily resurrection and second advent, they went aside from the saving doctrine of Jesus themselves, and were sure—which was worse—to make others go aside from it ten thousand times more. But they were too near to Jesus not to have been able to preserve the main lines of his teaching, to preserve his way of using words; and they did, in fact, preserve them.

The reason extra-beliefs flourished

But at their death the immediate remembrance of Jesus faded away, and whatever *Aberglaube* the apostles themselves had had and sanctioned was left to work without check. And, at the same time, the world and society presented conditions constantly less and less favourable to sane criticism. And it was then, and under these conditions, that the dogma which is now called orthodox, and which our dogmatic friends imagine to be purely a methodical arrangement of the admitted facts of Christianity, grew up. We have shown from the thing itself, by putting the dogma in comparison with the genuine teaching of Jesus, how little it is this; but it is well to make clear to oneself, also (for one can) , from the circumstances of the case, that it *could* not be this.

For dogmatic theology is, in fact, an attempt at both literary and scientific criticism of the highest order; and the age which developed dogma had neither the resources nor the faculty for such a criticism. It is idle to talk of the theological instinct, the analogy of faith, as if by the mere occupation with a limited subject-matter one could reach the truth about it. It is as if one imagined that by the mere study of Greek we could reach the truth about the origin of Greek words, and dogmatise about them; and could appeal to our supposed possession, through our labours, of the philological instinct, the analogy of language, to make our dogmatism go down. In general such an instinct, whether theological or philological, will mean merely, that, having accustomed ourselves to look at things through a glass of a certain colour, we see them always of that colour. What the science of Bible-criticism, like all other science, needs, is a very wide experience from comparative observation in many directions, and a very slowly acquired habit of mind. All studies have the benefit of these guides, when they exist, and one isolated study can never have the benefit of them by itself. There is a common order, a general level, an uniform possibility, for these things. As were the geography, history, physiology, cosmology, of the men who developed dogma, so was also their faculty for a scientific Bible-criticism, such as dogma pretends to be. Now we know what their geography, history, physiology, cosmology, were. Cosmas Indicopleustes, a Christian navigator of Justinian's time, denies that the earth is spherical, and asserts it to be a flat surface with the sky put over it like a dish cover. The Christian metaphysics of the same age applying the ideas of substance and identity to what the Bible says about God, Jesus, and the Holy Spirit, are on a par with this natural philosophy.

And again, as one part of their scientific Bible-criticism, so the rest. We have seen in the Bible-writers themselves a quite uncritical use of the Old Testament and of prophecy.

Now, does this become less in the authors of our dogmatic theology—a far more pretentious effort of criticism than the Bible-writers ever made—or does it become greater? It becomes a thousand times greater. Not only are definite predictions found where they do not exist—as, for example, in Isaiah's *I will restore thy judges as at the first*,[10] is found a definite foretelling of the Apostles—but in the whole Bible a secret allegorical sense is supposed, higher than the natural sense; so that Jerome calls tracing the natural sense an eating dust like the serpent, *in modum serpentis terram comedere.* Therefore, for one expounder, Isaiah's prophecy against Egypt: *The Eternal rideth upon a light cloud, and shall come into Egypt*,[11] is the flight into Egypt of the Holy Family, and the *light cloud* is the virgin-born body of Jesus; for another, *The government shall be upon his shoulder*,[12] is Christ's carrying upon his shoulder the cross; for another, *The lion shall eat straw like the ox*,[13] is the faithful and the wicked alike receiving the body of Christ in the Eucharist.

These are the men, this is the critical faculty, from which our so-called orthodox dogma proceeded. The worth of all the productions of such a critical faculty is easy to estimate, for the worth is nearly uniform. When the Rabbinical expounders interpret: *Woe unto them that lay field to field!* [14] as a prophetic curse on the accumulation of Church property, or: *Woe unto them that rise up early in the morning that they may follow strong drink!* [15] as a prediction of the profligacy of the Church clergy, or: *Woe unto them that draw iniquity with cords of vanity!* [16] as God's malediction on Church bells, we say at once that such critics thus give their measure as interpreters of the true sense of the Bible. The moment we think seriously and fairly, we must see that the Patristic interpretations of prophecy give, in like manner, their authors' measure as interpreters of the

[10] Isaiah 1:26.
[12] Isaiah 9:6.
[14] Isaiah 5:8.
[16] Isaiah 5:18.

[11] Isaiah 19:1.
[13] Isaiah 65:25.
[15] Isaiah 5:11.

true sense of the Bible. Yet this is what the dogma of the Nicene and Athanasian Creeds professes to be, and must be if it is to be worth anything—*the true sense extracted from the Bible*; for, "the Bible is the record of the whole revealed faith," says Cardinal Newman. But we see how impossible it is that this true sense the dogma of these creeds should be. . . .

The Schoolmen follow suit

The Schoolmen themselves are but the same false criticism developed, and clad in an apparatus of logic and system. In that grand and instructive repertory founded by the Benedictines, the *Histoire Littéraire de la France*, we read that in the theological faculty of the University of Paris, the leading mediaeval university, it was seriously discussed whether Jesus at his ascension had his clothes on or not. If he had not, did he appear before his apostles naked? if he had, what became of the clothes? *Monstrous!* everyone will say.[17] Yes, but the very same criticism, only full-blown, which produced: "Neither confounding the Persons nor dividing the Substance." The very same criticism, which originally treated terms as scientific which were not scientific; which, instead of applying literary and historical criticism to the data of popular *Aberglaube,* took these data just as they stood and merely dressed them scientifically.

Catholic dogma itself is true, urges, however, Cardinal Newman, because intelligent Catholics have dropped errors and absurdities like the False Decretals or the works of the pretended Dionysius the Areopagite, but have not dropped dogma. This is only saying that men drop the more palpable blunder before the less palpable. The adequate criticism of the Bible is extremely difficult, and slowly does the "Zeit-Geist" unveil it. Meanwhile, of the premature and

[17] Be it observed, however, that there is an honest scientific effort in the Schoolmen, and that to this sort of thing one really *does* come, when one fairly sets oneself to treat miracles literally and exactly; but most of us are content to leave them in a half light.

false criticism to which we are accustomed, we drop the evidently weak parts first; we retain the rest, to drop it gradually and piece by piece as it loosens and breaks up. But it is all of one order, and in time it will all go. Not the Athanasian Creed's damnatory clauses only, but the whole Creed; not this one Creed only, but the three Creeds—our whole received application of *science*, popular or learned, to the Bible. For it was an inadequate and false science, and could not, from the nature of the case, be otherwise.

3

And now we see how much that clergyman deceives himself, who writes to the *Guardian*: "The objectors to the Athanasian Creed at any rate admit, that its doctrinal portions are truly the carefully distilled essence of the scattered intimations of Holy Scripture on the deep mysteries in question—priceless discoveries made in that field." When one has travelled to the Athanasian Creed along the gradual line of the historical development of Christianity, instead of living stationary all one's life with this Creed blocking up the view, one is really tempted to say, when one reads a deliverance like that of this clergyman: *Sancta simplicitas!* It is just because the Athanasian Creed pretends to be, in its doctrine, "the carefully distilled essence of the scattered intimations of Holy Scripture," and *is so very far from it*, that it is worthless. . . . It is really a mixture—for true criticism, as it ripens, it is even a grotesque mixture—of learned pseudo-science with popular *Aberglaube*.

Our real difficulty with Scripture not intellectual but moral

But it cannot be too carefully borne in mind that the real "essence of Holy Scripture," its saving truth, is no such criticism at all as the so-called orthodox dogma attempts and attempts unsuccessfully. No, the real essence of Scripture is a much simpler matter. It is, for the Old Testament: *To him that ordereth his conversation right shall be shown the salvation of God!*—and, for the New Testament: *Follow Jesus!* This is Bible-dogma, as opposed to the dogma of our formularies. On this Bible-dogma if Churches were founded, and to preach this Bible-dogma if ministers were ordained, Churches and ministers would have all the dogma to which the Bible attaches eternal life. Plain and precise enough it is, in all conscience; with the advantage of being precisely *right*, whereas the dogma of our formularies is precisely *wrong*. And if anyone finds it too simple, let him remember that its hardness is practical, not speculative. It is a rule of *conduct*; let him act it, and he will find it hard enough. *Utinam per unum diem bene essemus conversati in hoc mundo!* * But as a matter of mere knowledge it is very simple, it lies on the surface of the Bible and cannot be missed. . . .

And from time to time, through the course of ages, there have arisen men who threw themselves on the method and secret of Jesus with extraordinary force, with intuitive sense that here was salvation; and who really cared for nothing else, though ecclesiastical dogma, too, they professed to believe, and sincerely thought they did believe—but their heart was elsewhere. These are they who "received the kingdom of God as a little child," who perceived how simple a thing Christianity was, though so inexhaustible, and who are therefore "the greatest in the kingdom of God." And they, not the theological doctors, are the true lights of the Christian Church; not Augustine, Luther, Bossuet, Butler, but the nameless author of the *Imitation*, but Tauler, but St. Francis of Sales, Wilson of Sodor and Man. Yet not only these men, but the whole body of Christian churches and sects always, have all at least *professed* the method and

* Thomas á Kempis, *The Imitation of Christ,* I. xxiii, 2: "Would that for one single day we had lived in this world as we ought."—*Ed.*

secret of Jesus, and to some extent used them. And when-
ever these were used, they have borne their natural fruits of
joy and life; and this joy and this life have been taken to
flow from the ecclesiastical dogma held along with them,
and to sanction and prove it. And people, eager to praise
the bridge which carried them over from death to life, have
taken this dogma for the bridge, or part of the bridge, that
carried them over, and have eagerly praised it. Thus religion has been made to stand on its apex instead of its base.
Righteousness is supported on ecclesiastical dogma, instead
of ecclesiastical dogma being supported on righteousness.

But in the beginning it was not so. Because righteousness is eternal, necessary, life-giving, *therefore* the mighty
"not ourselves which makes for righteousness" was the Eternal, Israel's God; was all-powerful, all-merciful; sends his
Messiah, elects his people, establishes his kingdom, receives
into everlasting habitations. But gradually this petrifies,
gradually it is more and more added to; until at last, because righteousness was originally perceived to be eternal,
necessary, life-giving, we find ourselves "worshipping One
God in Trinity and Trinity in Unity, neither confounding
the Persons nor dividing the Substance." And then the original order is reversed. Because there is One God in Trinity
and Trinity in Unity, who receives into everlasting habitations, establishes his kingdom, elects his people, sends his
Messiah, is all-merciful, all-powerful, Israel's God, the Eternal—*therefore* righteousness is eternal, necessary, life-giving.
And shake the belief in the One God in Trinity and Trinity in Unity, the belief in righteousness is shaken, it is
thought, also. Whereas righteousness and the God of righteousness, the God of the Bible, are in truth quite independent of the God of ecclesiastical dogma, the work of critics of
the Bible—critics understanding neither what they say nor
whereof they affirm.

4

So false, so astoundingly false (thus one is inclined to
say by the light which the "Zeit-Geist" is beginning to hold
out over them) are both popular and learned science in
their criticism of the Bible. And for the learned science one
feels no tenderness, because it has gone wrong with a great
parade of exactitude and philosophy; whereas all it really
did was to take the magnified and non-natural Man of popular religion as God, and to take Jesus as his son, and then
to state the relations between them metaphysically. No difficulties suggested by the popular science of religion has this
learned science ever removed, and it has created plenty of
its own.

The moral value of the popular science
of Christianity

But for the popular science of religion one has, or
ought to have, an infinite tenderness. It is the spontaneous
work of nature. It is the travail of the human mind to adapt
to its grasp and employment great ideas of which it feels the
attraction, but for which, except as given to it by this travail, it would have been immature. The imperfect science of
the Bible, formulated in the so-called Apostles' Creed, was
the only vehicle by which, to generation after generation of
men, the method and secret of Jesus could gain any access;
and in this sense we may even call it, taking the point of
view of popular theology, *providential*. And this rude criticism is full of poetry, and in this poetry we have been all
nursed. To call it, as many of our philosophical Liberal
friends are fond of calling it, "a degrading superstition," is
as untrue, as it is a poor compliment to human nature,
which produced this criticism and used it. It is an *Aberglaube*, or extra belief and fairy-tale, produced by taking
certain great names and great promises too literally and ma
terially; but it is *not* a degrading superstition.

Protestants, on their part, have no difficulty in calling the Catholic doctrine of the mass "a degrading superstition." It is indeed a rude and blind criticism of Jesus Christ's words: *He that eateth me shall live by me.* But once admit the miracle of the "atoning sacrifice," once move in this order of ideas, and what can be more natural and beautiful than to imagine this miracle every day repeated, Christ offered in thousands of places, everywhere the believer enabled to enact the work of redemption and unite himself with the Body whose sacrifice saves him? And the effect of this belief has been no more degrading than the belief itself. The fourth book of the *Imitation,* which treats of *The Sacrament of the Altar,* is of later date and lesser merit than the three books which precede it; but it is worth while to quote from it a few words for the sake of the testimony they bear to the practical operation, in many cases at any rate, of this belief. "To us in our weakness thou hast given, for the refreshment of mind and body, thy sacred Body. The devout communicant thou, my God, raisest from the depth of his own dejection to the hope of thy protection, and with a hitherto unknown grace renewest him and enlightenest him within; so that they who at first, before this Communion, had felt themselves distressed and affectionless, after the refreshment of this meat and drink from heaven find themselves changed to a new and better man. For this most high and worthy Sacrament is the saving health of soul and body, the medicine of all spiritual languor; *by it my vices are cured, my passions bridled, temptations are conquered or diminished, a larger grace is infused, the beginnings of virtue are made to grow, faith is confirmed, hope strengthened, and charity takes fire and dilates into flame.*" So little is the doctrine of the mass to be hastily called "a degrading superstition," either in its character or in its working.

But it is *false!* sternly breaks in the Evangelical Protestant. O Evangelical Protestant, is thine own doctrine, then, so true? As the Romish doctrine of the mass, "the Real Presence," is a rude and blind criticism of, *He that eateth*

me shall live by me;[18] so the Protestant tenet of justification, "pleading the blood of the Covenant," is a rude and
blind criticism of, *The Son of Man came to give his life a
ransom for many.*[19] It is a taking of the words of Scripture
literally and unintelligently. And our friends, the philosophical Liberals, are not slow to call this, too, a degrading
superstition, just as Protestants call the doctrine of the mass
a degrading superstition. We say, on the contrary, that a
degrading superstition neither the one nor the other is. In
imagining a sort of supernatural man, a man infinitely magnified and improved, with a race of vile offenders to deal
with, whom his natural goodness would incline him to let
off, only his sense of justice will not allow it; then a younger
supernatural man, his son, on the scale of his father and
very dear to him, who might live in grandeur and splendour
if he liked, but who prefers to leave his home, to go and live
among the race of offenders, and to be put to an ignomin-
ious death, on condition that his merits shall be counted
against their demerits, and that his father's goodness shall
be restrained no longer from taking effect, but any offender
shall be admitted to the benefit of it on simply pleading the
satisfaction made by the son—and then, finally, a third
supernatural man, still on the same high scale, who keeps
very much in the background, and works in a very occult
manner, but very efficaciously nevertheless, and who is busy
in applying everywhere the benefits of the son's satisfaction,
and the father's goodness—in an imagination, I say, such as
this, there is nothing degrading, and this is precisely the
Protestant story of *Justification.* And how awe of the first of
these supernatural persons, gratitude and love towards the
second, and earnest co-operation with the third, may fill and
rule men's hearts so as to transform their conduct, we need
not go about to show, for we have all seen it with our eyes.
Therefore in the practical working of this tenet there is
nothing degrading; any more than there is anything degrad-

[18] John 6:57.   [19] Matthew 20:28.

ing in the tenet as an imaginative conception. And looking to the infinite importance of getting right conduct—three-fourths of human life—established, and to the inevitable anthropomorphism and *extra-belief* of men in dealing with ideas, one might well hesitate to attack an anthropomorphism or an extra-belief by which men helped themselves in conduct, merely because an anthropomorphism or an extra-belief it is, so long as it served its purpose, so long as it was firmly and undoubtingly held, and almost universally prevailing.

But, after all, the question sooner or later arises in respect to a matter taken for granted, like the Catholic doctrine of the Mass or the Protestant doctrine of Justification: Is it *sure?* can what is here assumed be *verified?* And this is the real objection both to the Catholic and to the Protestant doctrine as a basis for conduct—not that it is a degrading superstition, but that it is *not sure;* that it assumes what cannot be *verified.*

For a long time this objection occurred to scarcely anybody. And there are still, and for a long time yet there will be, many to whom it does not occur. In particular, on those "devout women" who in the history of religion have continually played a part in many respects so beautiful but in some respects so mischievous—on them, and on a certain number of men like them, it has and can as yet have, so far as one can see, no effect at all. . . .

Arbitrary and unsupported, however, as the story they have taken up with may be, yet it puts them in connexion with the Bible and the religion of the Bible—that is, with righteousness and with the method and secret of Jesus. These are so clear in the Bible that no one who uses it can help seeing them there; and of these they do take for their use something, though on a wrong ground. But these, so far as they are taken into use, are saving.

Chapter X

Our "Masses" and the Bible

1

Many, however, and of a much stronger and more important sort, there now are, who will not thus take on trust the story which is made the reason for putting ourselves in connexion with the Bible and learning to use its religion; be it the story of the divine authority of the Church, as in Catholic countries, or—as generally with us—the story of the three supernatural persons standing on its own merits. Is what this story asserts *true*, they are beginning to ask; can it be verified?—since experience proves, they add, that whatever for man is true, man can verify. And certainly the fairy-tale of the three supernatural persons no man can verify. They find this to be so, and then they say: The Bible takes for granted this story and depends on the truth of it; what, then, can rational people have to do with the Bible? So they get rid, to be sure, of a false ground for using the Bible, but they at the same time lose the Bible itself, and the true religion of the Bible: righteousness, and the method and secret of Jesus. And those who lose this are *the masses*, as they are called; or rather they are what is most strenuous, intelligent, and alive among the masses, and what will give the signal for the rest to follow.

*The masses are following the cultivated
in rejecting the Bible*

This is what everyone sees to constitute the special moral feature of our times: *the masses* are losing the Bible and its religion. At the Renascence, many cultivated wits lost it; but the great solid mass of the common people kept

135

it, and brought the world back to it after a start had seemed to be made in quite another direction. But now it is *the people* which is getting detached from the Bible. The masses can no longer be relied on to counteract what the cultivated wits are doing, and stubbornly to make clever men's extravagances and aberrations, if about the Bible they commit them, of no avail. When our philosophical Liberal friends say, that by universal suffrage, public meetings, Church-disestablishment, marrying one's deceased wife's sister, secular schools, industrial development, man can very well live; and that if he studies the writings, say, of Mr. Herbert Spencer into the bargain, he will be perfect, he "will have in modern and congenial language the truisms common to all systems of morality," and the Bible is become quite old-fashioned and superfluous for him—when our philosophical friends now say this, the masses, far from checking them, are disposed to applaud them to the echo. Yet assuredly, of conduct, which is more than three-fourths of human life, the Bible, whatever people may thus think and say, is the great inspirer; so that from the great inspirer of more than three-fourths of human life the masses of our society seem now to be cutting themselves off. This promises, certainly, if it does not already constitute, a very unsettled condition of things. And the cause of it lies in the Bible being made to depend on a story, or set of asserted facts, which it is impossible to verify; and which hard-headed people, therefore, treat as either an imposture, or a fairy-tale that discredits all which is found in connexion with it.

2

The conception of God the crux of the problem

Now if we look attentively at the story, or set of asserted but unverified and unverifiable facts, which we have summarised in popular language above, and which is alleged as the basis of the Bible, we shall find that the difficulty really lies all in one point. The whole difficulty is with the infinitely magnified man who is the first of the three supernatural persons of our story. If *he* could be verified, the data we have are, possibly, enough to warrant our admitting the truth of the rest of the story. It is singular how few people seem to see this, though it is really quite clear. The Bible is supposed to assume a great Personal First Cause, who thinks and loves, the moral and intelligent Governor of the Universe. This is the God, also, of *natural religion*, as people call it; and this supposed certainty learned reasoners take, and render it more certain still by considerations of causality, identity, existence, and so on. These, however, are not found to help the certainty much; but a certainty in itself the Great Personal First Cause, the God of both natural and revealed religion, is supposed to be.

Then, to this given beginning, all that the Bible delivers has to fit itself on. And so arises the account of the God of the Old Testament, and of Christ and of the Holy Ghost, and of the incarnation and atonement, and of the sacraments, and of inspiration, and of the church, and of eternal punishment and eternal bliss, as theology presents them. But difficulties strike people in this or that of these doctrines. The incarnation seems incredible to one, the vicarious atonement to another, the real presence to a third, inspiration to a fourth, eternal punishment to a fifth, and so on. And they set to work to make religion more pure and rational, as they suppose, by pointing out that this or that of these doctrines is false, that it must be a mistake of theologians; and by interpreting the Bible so as to show that the doctrine is not really there. The Unitarians are, perhaps, the great people for this sort of partial and local rationalising of religion; for taking what here and there on the surface seems to conflict most with common sense, arguing that it cannot be in the Bible and getting rid of it, and professing to have thus relieved religion of its difficulties. And now, when there is much loosening of authority and tradition, much impatience of what conflicts with common sense, the

Unitarians are beginning confidently to give themselves out as the Church of the Future.

But in all this there is in reality a good deal of what we must call intellectual shallowness. For, granted that there are things in a system which are puzzling, yet they belong to a *system;* and it is childish to pick them out by themselves and reproach them with error, when you leave untouched the basis of the system where they occur, and indeed admit it for sound yourself. The Unitarians are very loud about the unreasonableness and unscripturalness of the common doctrine of the Atonement. But in the Socinian Catechism it stands written: "It is necessary for salvation to know that God *is;* and to know that God is, is to be firmly persuaded that there exists in reality some One, who has supreme dominion over all things." Presently afterwards it stands written, that among the testimonies to Christ are, "miracles very great and immense," *miracula admodum magna et immensa.* Now, with the One Supreme Governor, and miracles, given to start with, it may fairly be urged that that construction put by common theology on the Bible-data, which we call the story of the three supernatural men, and in which the Atonement fills a prominent place, is the natural and legitimate construction to put on them, and not unscriptural at all. Neither is it unreasonable; in a system of things, that is, where the Supreme Governor and miracles, or even where the Supreme Governor without miracles, are already given.

And this is Butler's great argument in the *Analogy.* You all concede, he says to his deistical adversaries, a Supreme Personal First Cause, the almighty and intelligent Governor of the universe; this, you and I both agree, is the system and order of nature. But you are offended at certain things in revelation—that is, at things, Butler means, like a future life with rewards and punishments, or like the doctrine of the Trinity as theology collects it from the Bible. Well, I will show you, he says, that in your and my admitted system of nature there are just as great difficulties as in the system of revelation. And he does show it; and by adversaries such as his, who grant what the Deist or Socinian grants, he never has been answered, he never can be answered. The spear of Butler's reasoning will even follow and transfix the Duke of Somerset, who finds so much to condemn in the Bible, but "retires into one unassailable fortress—faith in God."

The only question, perhaps, is, whether Butler, as an Anglican bishop, puts an adequate construction upon what Bible revelation, this basis of the Supreme Personal First Cause being supposed, may be allowed to be; whether Catholic dogma is not the truer construction to put upon it. Cardinal Newman urges, fairly enough: Butler admits, analogy is in some sort violated by the fact of revelation; only, with the precedent of natural religion given, we have to own that the difficulties against revelation are not greater than against this precedent, and therefore the admission of this precedent of natural religion may well be taken to clear them. And must we not go farther in the same way, asks Cardinal Newman, and own that the precedent of revelation, too, may be taken to cover more than itself; and that as, the Supreme Governor being given, it is credible that the Incarnation is true, so, the Incarnation being true, it is credible that God should not have left the world to itself after Christ and his Apostles disappeared, but should have lodged divine insight in the Church and its visible head? So pleads Cardinal Newman; and if it be said that facts are against the infallibility of the Church, or that Scripture is against it, yet to wide, immense things, like facts and Scripture, a turn may easily be given which makes them favour it; and so an endless field for discussion is opened, and no certain conclusion is possible. For, once launched on this line of hypothesis and inference, with a Supreme Governor assumed, and the task thrown upon us of making out what he means us to infer and what we may suppose him to do and to intend, one of us may infer one thing and another of us another, and neither can possibly prove himself to be right or his adversary to be wrong.

The masses require a plain, experimental proof

Only, there may come some one, who says that the basis of all our inference, the Supreme Personal First Cause, the moral and intelligent Governor, is *not* the order of nature, is an assumption, and not a fact; and then, if this is so, our whole superstructure falls to pieces like a house of cards. And this is just what is happening at present. The masses, with their rude practical instinct, go straight to the heart of the matter. They are told there is a great Personal First Cause, who thinks and loves, the moral and intelligent Author and Governor of the universe; and that the Bible and Bible-righteousness come to us from him. Now, they do not begin by asking, with the intelligent Unitarian, whether the doctrine of the Atonement is worthy of this moral and intelligent Ruler; they begin by asking what proof we have of him at all. Moreover, they require proof which is clear and certain; demonstration, or else plain experimental proof, such as that fire burns them if they touch it. If they are to study and obey the Bible because it comes from the Personal First Cause who is Governor of the universe, they require to be able to ascertain that there *is* this Governor, just as they are able to ascertain that the angles of a triangle are equal to two right angles, or that fire burns. And if they cannot ascertain it, they will let the intelligent Unitarian perorate for ever about the Atonement if he likes, but they themselves pitch the whole Bible to the winds.

Now, it is remarkable what a resting on mere probabilities, or even on less than probabilities, the proof for religion comes, in the hands of its great apologist, Butler, to be, even after he has started with the assumption of his moral and intelligent Governor. And no wonder; for in the primary assumption itself there is and can be nothing demonstrable or experimental, and therefore clearly known. So that of Christianity, as Butler grounds it, the natural criti-

cism would really be in these words of his own: "Supposi-
tions are not to be looked upon as true, because not incredible." However, Butler maintains that in matters of practice, such as religion, this is not incredible. Even the doubt-
ing about religion implies, he argues, that it *may* be true.
Now, in matters of practice we are bound in prudence, he
says, to act upon what may be a low degree of evidence; yes,
*"even though it be so low as to leave the mind in very great
doubt what is the truth."*

Was there ever such a way of establishing righteousness
heard of? And suppose we tried this with rude, hard, downright people, with the masses, who for what is told them
want, above all, a plain experimental proof, such as that fire
will burn you if you touch it. Whether in prudence they
ought to take the Bible and religion on a low degree of
evidence, or not, it is quite certain that on this ground they
never *will* take them. And it is quite certain, moreover, that
never on this ground did Israel, from whom we derive our
religion, take it himself or recommend it. He did not take it
in prudence, because he found at any rate a low degree of
evidence for it; he took it in rapture, because he found for it
an evidence irresistible. But his own words are the best:
"Thou, O Eternal, art the thing that I long for, thou art my
hope even from my youth: through thee have I been holden
up ever since I was born.[1] The statutes of the Eternal rejoice the heart; more desirable they are than gold, sweeter
than honey; in keeping of them there is great reward.[2] The
Eternal is my strength, my heart hath trusted in him and I
am helped; therefore my heart danceth for joy, and in my
song will I praise him." [3] That is why Israel took his
religion.

[1] Psalms 71:5–6.   [2] Psalms 19:8, 10, 11.
[3] Psalms 28:7.

3

But if Israel spoke of the Eternal thus, it was, we say, because he had a plain experimental proof of him. God was to Israel neither an assumption nor a metaphysical idea; he was a power that can be verified as much as the power of fire to burn or of bread to nourish: *the power, not ourselves, that makes for righteousness.* And the greatness of Israel in religion, the reason why he is said to have had religion revealed to him, to have been entrusted with the oracles of God, is because he had in such extraordinary force and vividness the perception of this power. And he communicates it irresistibly because he feels it irresistibly; that is why the Bible is not as other books that inculcate righteousness. Israel speaks of his intuition still feeling it to be an intuition, an experience; not as something which others have delivered to him, nor yet as a piece of metaphysical notion-building. Anthropomorphic he is, for all men are, and especially men not endowed with the Aryan genius for abstraction; but he does not make arbitrary assertions which can never be verified, like our popular religion, nor is he ever pseudo-scientific, like our learned religion.

Israel not speculative

He is credited with the metaphysical ideas of the personality of God, of the unity of God, and of creation as opposed to evolution; ideas depending, the first two of them, on notions of essence, existence, and identity, the last of them on the notion of cause and design. But he is credited with them falsely. All the countenance he gives to the metaphysical idea of the personality of God is given by his anthropomorphic language, in which, being a man himself, he naturally speaks of the Power, with which he is concerned, as a man also. So he says that Moses saw God's hinder parts;[4] and he gives just as much countenance to the scientific assertion that God has hinder parts, as to the scientific assertion of God's personality. That is, he gives no countenance at all to either. As to his asserting the unity of God the case is the same. He would give, indeed, his heart and his worship to no manifestation of power, except of the power which makes for *righteousness*; but he affords to the metaphysical idea of the unity of God no more countenance than this, and this is none at all. Then, lastly, as to the idea of creation. He viewed, indeed, all order as depending on the supreme order of righteousness, and all the fulness and beauty of the world as a boon added to the stock of that holder of the greatest of all boons already, the righteous. This, however, is as much countenance as he gives to the famous argument from design, or to the doctrine of creation as opposed to evolution. And it is none at all.

Free as is his use of anthropomorphic language, Israel had, as we have remarked already, far too keen a sense of reality not to shrink, when he comes anywhere near to the notion of exact speaking about God, from affirmation, from professing to know a whit more than he does know. "Lo, these are skirts of his ways," he says of what he has experienced, *"but how little a portion is known of him!"* [5] And again: *"The secret things belong unto the Eternal our God;* but the revealed things belong unto us and to our children for ever: that we may do all the words of this law." [6] How different from our licence of full and particular statement: "A Personal First Cause, who thinks and loves, the moral and intelligent Governor of the universe!" Israel knew, concerning the eternal *not ourselves*, that it was "a power that made for righteousness." This was revealed to Israel and his children, and through them to the world; all the rest about the eternal *not ourselves* was this power's own secret. And all Israel's language about this power, except that *it makes*

[4] Exodus 33:23.   [5] Job 26:14.
[6] Deuteronomy 29:29.

for righteousness, is approximate language—the language of poetry and eloquence, thrown out at a vast object of our consciousness not fully apprehended by it, but extending infinitely beyond it.

This, however, was "a revealed thing," Israel said, to him and to his children: "the Eternal not ourselves that makes for righteousness." And now, then, let us go to the masses with what Israel really did say, instead of what our popular and our learned religion may choose to make him say. Let us announce, not: "There rules a Great Personal First Cause, who thinks and loves, the moral and intelligent Governor of the universe, and *therefore* study your Bible and learn to obey this!" No; but let us announce: "There rules an enduring Power, not ourselves, which makes for righteousness, and *therefore* study your Bible and learn to obey this." For if we announce the other instead, and they reply: "First let us *verify* that there rules a Great Personal First Cause, who thinks and loves, the moral and intelligent Governor of the universe"—what are we to answer? We *cannot* answer.

*The Power not ourselves which makes
for righteousness verifiable*

But if, on the other hand, they ask: "How are we to *verify* that there rules an enduring Power, not ourselves, which makes for righteousness?"—we may answer at once: "How? why as you verify that fire burns—by experience! It *is* so; try it! you *can* try it; every case of conduct, of that which is more than three-fourths of your own life and of the life of all mankind, will prove it to you! Disbelieve it, and you will find out your mistake as surely as, if you disbelieve that fire burns and put your hand into the fire, you will find out your mistake! Believe it, and you will find the benefit of it!" This is the first experience.

But then the masses may go on, and say: "Why, however, even if there *is* an enduring Power, not ourselves, that makes for righteousness, should we study the *Bible* that we may learn to obey him?—will not other teachers or books do as well?" And here again the answer is: "Why?—why, because this Power is *revealed* in Israel and the Bible, and not by other teachers and books! that is, there is infinitely more of him there, he is plainer and easier to come at, and incomparably more impressive. If you want to know plastic art, you go to the Greeks; if you want to know science, you go to the Aryan genius. And why? Because they have the specialty for these things; for making us feel what they are and giving us an enthusiasm for them. Well, and so have Israel and the Bible a specialty for righteousness, for making us feel what it is and giving us an enthusiasm for it. And here again it is experience that we invoke: *try it!* Having convinced yourself that there is an enduring Power, not ourselves, that makes for righteousness, set yourself next to try to learn more about this Power, and to feel an enthusiasm for it. And to this end, take a course of the Bible first, and then a course of Benjamin Franklin, Horace Greeley, Jeremy Bentham, and Mr. Herbert Spencer; see which has most effect, which satisfies you most, which gives you most moral force. Why, the Bible is of such avail for teaching righteousness, that even to those who come to it with all sorts of false notions about the God of the Bible, it yet does teach righteousness, and fills them with the love of it; how much more those who come to it with a *true* notion about the God of the Bible!" And this is the second experience. . . .

4

That Jesus is the Son of God also verifiable

Suppose the Bible is discovered, when its expressions are rightly understood, to start with an assertion which *can* be verified: the assertion, namely, not of "a Great Personal First Cause," but of "an enduring Power, not ourselves, that makes for righteousness." Then by the light of this discovery we read and understand all the expressions that follow.

Jesus comes forth from this enduring Power that makes for righteousness, is sent by this Power, is this Power's Son; the Holy Spirit proceeds from this same Power, and so on.

Now, from the innumerable minor difficulties which attend the story of the three supernatural men, this right construction, put on what the Bible says of Jesus, of the Father, and of the Holy Spirit, is free. But it is free from the major difficulty also; for it neither depends upon what is unverifiable, nor is it unverifiable itself. That Jesus *is* the Son of a Great Personal First Cause is itself unverifiable; and that there *is* a Great Personal First Cause is unverifiable too. But that there is an enduring Power, nor ourselves, which makes for righteousness, is verifiable, as we have seen, by experience; and that Jesus *is* the offspring of this Power is verifiable from experience also. For God is the author of righteousness; now, Jesus is the Son of God because he gives the method and secret by which alone is righteousness possible. And that he *does* give this, we can verify, again, from experience. It *is* so! try, and you will find it to be so! Try all the ways to righteousness you can think of, and you will find that no way brings you to it except the way of Jesus, but that this way does bring you to it! And, therefore, as we found we could say to the masses: "Attempt to do without Israel's God that makes for righteousness, and you will find out your mistake!" so we find we can now proceed farther, and say: "Attempt to reach righteousness by any way except that of Jesus, and you will find out your mistake!" This is a thing that *can* prove itself, if it is so; and it *will* prove itself, because it is so.

Thus, we have the authority of both Old and New Testament placed on just the same solid basis as the authority of the injunction to take food and rest: namely, that experience proves we cannot do without them. And we have neglect of the Bible punished just as putting one's hand into the fire is punished: namely, by finding we are the worse for it. Only, to *attend* to this experience about the Bible, needs more steadiness than to attend to the momentary impressions of hunger, fatigue, and pain; therefore it is called *faith,* and counted a virtue. But the appeal is to experience in this case just as much as in the other; only to experience of a far deeper and greater kind.

5

Reason and experience the only proper guides

So there is no doubt that we get a much firmer, nay an impregnable, ground for the Bible, and for recommending it to the world, if we put the construction on it which we propose. The only question is: Is this the *right* construction to put on it? is it the construction which properly belongs to the Bible? And here, again, our appeal is to the same test which we have employed throughout, the only possible test for man to employ—the test of reason and experience. Given the Bible-documents, what, it is inquired, is the right construction to put upon them? Is it the construction we propose? or is it the construction of the theologians, according to which the dogmas of the Trinity, the Incarnation, the Atonement, and so on, are presupposed all through the Bible, are sometimes latent, sometimes come more visibly to the surface, but are always there; and to them every word in the Bible has reference, plain or figured?

Now, the Bible does not and cannot tell us itself, in black and white, what is the right construction to put upon it; we have to make this out. And the only possible way to make it out—for the dogmatists to make out their construction, or for us to make out ours—is by reason and experience. "Even such as are readiest," says Hooker very well, "to cite for one thing five hundred sentences of Scripture, what warrant have they that any one of them doth mean the thing for which it is alleged?" They can have none, he replies, but reasoning and collection; and to the same effect Butler says of reason, that "it is indeed the only faculty we have wherewith to judge concerning *anything,* even revelation itself." Now it is simply from experience of the human spirit and its productions, from observing as widely as we can the manner in which men have thought, their way of using words and what they mean by them, and from reasoning upon this observation and experience, that we conclude the construction theologians put upon the Bible to be false, and ours to be the truer one. . . .

Demonstration in these matters is impossible. It is a maintainable thesis that the allegorising of the Fathers is right, and that this is the true sense of the Bible. It is a maintainable thesis that the theological dogmas of the Trinity, the Incarnation, and the Atonement, underlie the whole Bible. It is a maintainable thesis, also, that Jesus was himself immersed in the *Aberglaube* of his nation and time, and that his disciples have reported him with absolute fidelity; in this case we should have, in our estimate of Jesus, to make deductions for his *Aberglaube*, and to admire him for the insight he displayed in spite of it. This thesis, we repeat, or that thesis, or another thesis, is *maintainable*, as to the construction to be put on such a document as the Bible. Absolute demonstration is impossible, and the only question is: Does experience, as it widens and deepens, make for this or that thesis, or make against it? And the great thing against any such thesis as either of the two we have just mentioned is, that the more we know of the history of the human spirit and its deliverances, the more we have reason to think such a thesis improbable, and it loses its hold on our assent more. On the other hand, the great things, as we believe, in favour of such a contruction as we put upon the Bible is, that experience, as it increases, constantly confirms it; and that, though it cannot *command* assent, it will be found to *win* assent more and more. . . .

Chapter XI

The True Greatness
of Christianity

1

The grandeur of Christianity and the imposing and impressive attestation of it, if we could but worthily bring the thing out, is here: in that immense experimental proof of the necessity of it, which the whole course of the world has steadily accumulated, and indicates to us as still continuing and extending. Men will not admit assumptions, the popular legend they call a fairy-tale, the metaphysical demonstrations do not demonstrate, nothing but experimental proof will go down; and here is an experimental proof which never fails, and which at the same time is infinitely grander, by the vastness of its scale, the scope of its duration, the gravity of its results, than the machinery of the popular fairy-tale. Walking on the water, multiplying loaves, raising corpses, a heavenly judge appearing with trumpets in the clouds while we are yet alive—what is this compared to the real experience offered as witness to us by Christianity? It is like the difference between the grandeur of an extravaganza and the grandeur of the sea or the sky—immense objects which dwarf us, but where we are in contact with reality, and a reality of which we can gradually, though very slowly, trace the laws. . . .

Now, just as the best recommendation of the oracle committed to Israel, *Righteousness is salvation,* is found in our more and more discovering, in our own history and in the whole history of the world, that it *is* so, so we shall find it to be with the method and secret of Jesus. That this *is* the righteousness which is salvation, that the method and secret of Jesus, that is to say, conscience and self-renouncement, *are* righteousness, bring about the kingdom of God or the reign of righteousness—this, which is the Christian revelation and what Jesus came to establish, is best impressed, for the present at any rate, by experiencing and showing again and again, in ourselves and in the course of the world, that it *is* so; that this is the righteousness which is saving, and that none other saves. Let us but well observe what comes, in ourselves or the world, of trying any other, of not being convinced that this is righteousness, and this only; and we shall find ourselves more and more, as by irresistible viewless hands, caught and drawn towards the Christian revelation, and made to desire more and more to serve it. No proof can be so solid as this experimental proof; and none again, can be so grand, so fitted to fill us with awe, admiration, and gratitude. So that feeling and emotion will now well come in after it, though not before it. For the whole course of human things is really, according to this experience, leading up to the fulfilment of Jesus Christ's promise to his disciples: *Fear not, little flock! for it is your Father's good pleasure to give you the kingdom.*[1] And thus that comes out, after all, to be true, which St. Paul announced prematurely to the first generation of Christians: *When Christ, who is our life, shall appear, then shall ye also appear with him in glory.*[2] And the author of the Apocalypse, in like manner, foretold: *The kingdom of the world is become the kingdom of our Lord and his Christ.*[3] The kingdom of the Lord the world is already become, by its chief nations professing the religion of righteousness. The kingdom of Christ the world will have to become, it is on its way to become, because the profession of righteousness, except as Jesus Christ interpreted righteousness, is vain. We can see the process, we are ourselves part of it, and can in our measure help forward or keep back its completion.

When the prophet, indeed, says to Israel, on the point

[1] Luke 12:32.   [2] Colossians 3:4.
[3] Revelation 11:15. The Alexandrian manuscript is followed.

of being restored by Cyrus: *"The nation and kingdom that will not serve thee shall perish!"* [4] the promise, applied literally, fails. But extended to that idea of righteousness, of which Israel was the depositary and in which the real life of Israel lay, the promise is true, and we can see it fulfilled. In like manner, when the Apostle says to the Corinthians or to the Colossians, instructed that the second advent would come in their own generation *"We must all appear before the judgment-seat of Christ!"*[5]—*"When Christ, who is our life, shall appear, then shall ye also appear with him in glory!"* [6] the promise, applied literally as the Apostle meant it and his converts understood it, fails. But divested of this *Aberglaube* or extra-belief, it is true; if indeed the world can be shown—and it can—to be moving necessarily towards the triumph of that Christ in whom the Corinthian and Colossian disciples lived, and whose triumph is the triumph of all his disciples also.

2

The aspiration after immortality

Let us keep hold of this same experimental process in dealing with the promise of immortality; although here, if anywhere, *Aberglaube*, extra-belief, hope, anticipation, may well be permitted to come in. Still, what we need for our foundation is not *Aberglaube*, but *Glaube*; not extra-belief in what is beyond the range of possible experience, but belief in what can and should be known to be true.

By what futilities the demonstration of our immortality may be attempted, is to be seen in Plato's *Phaedo*. Man's natural desire for continuance, however little it may be worth as a scientific proof of our immortality, is at least a proof a thousand times stronger than any such demonstra-

---

[4] Isaiah 60:12.   [5] II Corinthians 5:10.
[6] Colossians 3:4.

tion. The want of solidity in such argument is so palpable, that one scarcely cares to turn a steady regard upon it at all. And even of the common Christian conception of immortality the want of solidity is, perhaps, most conclusively shown, by the impossibility of so framing it as that it will at all support a steady regard turned upon it. In our English popular religion, for instance, the common conception of a future state of bliss is just that of the Vision of Mirza: "Persons dressed in glorious habits with garlands on their heads, passing among the trees, lying down by the fountains, or resting on beds of flowers, amid a confused harmony of singing birds, falling waters, human voices, and musical instruments." Or, even, with many, it is that of a kind of perfected middle-class home, with labour ended, the table spread, goodness all around, the lost ones restored, hymnody incessant. *"Poor fragments all of this low earth!"* Keble might well say. That this conception of immortality cannot possibly be true, we feel, the moment we consider it seriously. And yet who can devise any conception of a future state of bliss, which shall bear close examination better?

Here, again, it is far best to take what is experimentally true, and nothing else, as our foundation, and afterwards to let hope and aspiration grow, if so it may be, out of this. Israel had said: "In the way of righteousness is life, and in the pathway thereof there is no death." [7] He had said: "The righteous hath hope in his death." [8] He had cried to his *Eternal that loveth righteousness*: "Thou wilt not leave my soul in the grave, neither wilt thou suffer they faithful servant to see corruption! thou wilt show me the path of life!" [9] And by a kind of short cut to the conclusion thus laid down, the Jews constructed their fairy-tale of an advent, judgment, and resurrection, as we find it in the Book of Daniel. Jesus, again, had said: "If a man keep my word, he shall never see death." [10] And by a kind of short cut to the

[7] Proverbs 12:28.   [8] Proverbs 14:32.
[9] Psalms 16:10–11.   [10] John 8:51.

conclusion thus laid down, Christians constructed their fairy-tale of the second advent, the resurrection of the body, the New Jerusalem. But instead of fairy-tales, let us begin, at least, with certainties.

And a certainty is the sense of *life*, of being truly *alive*, which accompanies righteousness. If this experimental sense does not rise to be stronger in us, does not rise to the sense of being inextinguishable, that is probably because our experience of righteousness is really so very small. Here, therefore, we may well permit ourselves to trust Jesus, whose practice and intuition both of them went, in these matters, so far deeper than ours. At any rate, we have in our experience this strong sense of *life from righteousness* to start with; capable of being developed, apparently, by progress in righteousness into something immeasurably stronger. Here is the true basis for all religious aspiration after immortality. And it is an experimental basis; and therefore, as to grandeur, it is again, when compared with the popular *Aberglaube*, grand with all the superior grandeur, on a subject of the highest seriousness, of reality over fantasy.

At present, the fantasy hides the grandeur of the reality. But when all the *Aberglaube* of the second advent, with its signs in the sky, sounding trumpets and opening graves, is cleared away, then and not till then will come out the profound truth and grandeur of words of Jesus like these: "The hour is coming, when they that are in the graves shall hear the voice of the Son of God; and they that hear shall *live*." [11]

In the Bible alone do we catch Jesus's sweet reasonableness

Finally, and above all. As, for the right inculcation of righteousness, we need the inspiring words of Israel's love for it, that is, we need the Bible; so, for the right inculcation of the method and secret of Jesus, we need the *epieikeia*, the

[11] John 5:25.

sweet reasonableness, of Jesus. That is, in other words again, we need the *Bible*; for only through the Bible-records of Jesus can we get at his *epieikeia*. Even in these records, it is and can be presented but imperfectly; but only by reading and re-reading the Bible can we get at it at all.

Now, greatly as the failure, from the stress laid upon the pseudo-science of Church-dogma, to lay enough stress upon the method and secret of Jesus, has kept Christianity back from showing itself in its full power, it is probable that the failure to apply to the method and secret of Jesus, so far as these have at any rate been used, his sweet reasonableness or *epieikeia*—his temper—has kept it back even more. And the *infinite* of the religion of Jesus—its immense capacity for ceaseless progress and farther development—lies principally, perhaps, in the line of disengaging and keeping before our minds, more and more, his temper, and applying it to our use of his method and secret. For it is obvious from experience, how much our use of Jesus Christ's method and secret requires to be guided and governed by his temper of *epieikeia*. Indeed, without this, his method and secret seem of no use at all. The Flagellants imagined that they were employing his secret; and the Dissenters, with their "spirit of watchful jealousy," imagine that they are employing his method. To be sure, Mr. Bradlaugh imagines that the method and the secret of Jesus, nay, and Jesus himself too, are all baneful, and that the sooner we get rid of them the better. So far, then, the Flagellants and the Dissenters are in advance of Mr. Bradlaugh: they value Christianity, and they profess the method and secret of Jesus. But they employ them so ill, that one is tempted to say they might nearly as well be without them. And this is because they are wholly without his temper of sweet reasonableness, or *epieikeia*. Now this can only be got, first, by knowing that it is in the Bible, and looking for it there; and then, by reading and re-reading the Gospels continually, until we catch something of it.

This, again, is an experimental process. That the *epiei-*

keia or sweet reasonableness of Jesus may be brought to govern our use of his method and secret, and that it can and will make our use of his method and secret quite a different thing, is proved by our actually finding this to be so when we try. So that the culmination of Christian righteousness, in the applying, to guide our use of the method and secret of Jesus, his sweet reasonableness or *epieikeia*, is proved from experience. We end, therefore, as we began—by experience. And the whole series of experiences, of which the survey is thus completed, rests primarily upon one fundamental fact —itself, eminently, a fact of experience: *the necessity of righteousness.*

Conclusion

1

Conduct requires culture

But now, after all we have been saying of the pre-eminency of righteousness, we remember what we have said formerly in praise of culture and of Hellenism, and against too much Hebraism, too exclusive a pursuit of the "one thing needful," as people call it. And we cannot help wondering whether we shall not be reproached with inconsistency, and told that we ought at least to sing, as the Greeks said, a *palinode;* and whether it may not really be so, and we ought. And, certainly, if we had ever said that Hellenism was three-fourths of human life, and conduct or righteousness but one-fourth, a palinode, as well as an unmusical man may, we would sing. But we have never said it. In praising culture, we have never denied that conduct, not culture, is three-fourths of human life.

Only it certainly appears, when the thing is examined, that conduct comes to have relations of a very close kind with culture. And the reason seems to be given by some words of our Bible, which, though they may not be exactly the right rendering of the original in that place, yet in themselves they explain the connexion of culture with conduct very well. "I have seen the travail," says the Preacher, "which God hath given to the sons of men to be exercised in it; he hath made everything beautiful in his time; also, he hath set the world in their heart." [1] *He hath set the world in their heart!*—that is why art and science, and what we

[1] Ecclesiastes 3:10–11.

call culture, are necessary. They may be only one-fourth of
man's life, but they are *there*, as well as the three-fourths
which conduct occupies. "He hath set *the world* in their
heart." And, really, the reason which we hence gather for
the close connexion between culture and conduct, is so
simple and natural that we are almost ashamed to give it;
but we have offered so many simple and natural explanations in place of the abstruse ones which are current, that
our hesitation is foolish.

Let us suggest then, that, having this one-fourth of
their nature concerned with art and science, men cannot
but somehow employ it. If they think that the three-fourths
of their nature concerned with conduct are the whole of
their nature, and that this is all they have to attend to, still
the neglected one-fourth is there, it ferments, it breaks
wildly out, it employs itself all at random and amiss. And
hence no doubt, our hymns and our dogmatic theology.
What is our dogmatic theology, except the mis-attribution
to the Bible—the Book of *conduct*—of a science and an
abstruse metaphysic which is not there, because our theologians have in themselves a faculty for science, for it makes
one-eighth of them? But they do not employ it on its proper
objects; so it invades the Bible, and tries to make the Bible
what it is not, and to put into it what is not there. And this
prevents their attending enough to what *is* in the Bible, and
makes them battle for what is *not* in the Bible, but they
have put it there!—battle for it in a manner clean contrary,
often, to the teaching of the Bible. So has arisen, for instance, all religious persecution. And thus, we say, has conduct itself become impaired.

So that conduct is impaired by the want of science and
culture; and our theologians really suffer, not from having
too much science, but from having too little. Whereas, if
they had turned their faculty for abstruse reasoning towards
the proper objects, and had given themselves, in addition, a
wide and large acquaintance with the productions of the
human spirit and with men's way of thinking and of using

words, then, on the one hand, they would not have been tempted to misemploy on the Bible their faculty for abstruse reasoning, for they would have had plenty of other exercise for it; and, on the other hand, they would have escaped that literary inexperience which now makes them fancy that the Bible-language is scientific, and fit matter for the application of their powers of abstruse reasoning to it, when it is no such thing. Then they would have seen the fallacy of confounding the obscurity attaching to the idea of God—that vast *not ourselves* which transcends us—with the obscurity attaching to the idea of their Trinity, a confused metaphysical speculation which puzzles us. The one, they would have perceived, is the obscurity of the immeasurable depth of air, the other is the obscurity of a fog. And fog, they would have known, has no proper place in our conceptions of God; since whatever our minds *can* possess of God they know clearly, for no man, as Goethe says, possesses what he does not understand; but they can possess of Him but a very little. All this our dogmatic theologians would have known, if they had had more science and more literature. And therefore, simple as the Bible and conduct are, still culture seems to be required for them—required to prevent our mis-handling and sophisticating them.

2

Culture will, finally, assist us
in forming a truer conception of God

Culture, then, and science and literature are requisite, in the interest of religion itself, even when, taking nothing but *conduct* into account, we rightly make the God of the Bible, as Israel made him, to be simply and solely "the Eternal Power, not ourselves, that makes for *righteousness.*" For we are not to forget, that, grand as this conception of God is, and well as it meets the wants of far the largest part of our being, of three-fourths of it, yet there is one-fourth of our being of which it does not strictly meet the wants, the part which is concerned with art and science; or, in other words, with beauty and exact knowledge

For the total man, therefore, the truer conception of God is as "the Eternal Power, not ourselves, by which all things fulfil the law of their being"; by which, therefore, we fulfil the law of our being so far as our being is aesthetic and intellective, as well as so far as it is moral. And it is evident, as we have before now remarked, that in this wider sense God is displeased and disserved by many things which cannot be said, except by putting a strain upon words, to displease and disserve him as the God of righteousness. He is displeased and disserved by men uttering such doggerel hymns as: *Sing glory, glory, glory to the great God Triune!* and: *Out of my stony griefs Bethels I'll raise!* and: *My Jesus to know, and feel his blood flow, 'tis life everlasting, 'tis heaven below!*—or by theologians uttering such pseudo-science as their *blessed truth that the God of the universe is a PERSON.* But it would be harsh to give, at present, this turn to our employment of the phrases, *pleasing God, displeasing God.*

And yet, as man makes progress, we shall surely come to doing this. For, the clearer our conceptions in science and art become, the more will they assimilate themselves to the conceptions of duty in conduct, will become practically stringent like rules of conduct, and will invite the same sort of language in dealing with them. And so far let us venture to poach on M. Émile Burnouf's manor, and to talk about the Aryan genius, as to say, that the love of art and science, and the energy and honesty in the pursuit of art and science, in the best of the Aryan races, do seem to correspond in a remarkable way to the love of conduct, and the energy and honesty in the pursuit of conduct, in the best of the Semitic. To treat science and art with the same kind of seriousness as conduct, does seem, therefore, to be a not impossible thing for the Aryan genius to come to.

But for all this, however, man is hardly yet ripe. For

our race, as we see it now and as ourselves we form a part of it, the true God is and must be pre-eminently the God of the Bible, *the Eternal who makes for righteousness*, from whom Jesus came forth, and whose Spirit governs the course of humanity. Only, we see that even for apprehending this God of the Bible rightly and not wrongly, science, and what so many people now disparage, letters, and what we call, in general, *culture*, seem to be necessary.

And meanwhile, to prevent our at all pluming our-selves on having apprehended what so much baffles our dog-matic friends (although indeed it is not so much we who apprehend it as the "Zeit-Geist" who discovers it to us), what a chastening and wholesome reflexion for us it is, that it is only to our natural inferiority to these ingenious men that we are indebted for our advantage over them! For while *they* were born with talents for metaphysical specula-tion and abstruse reasoning, we are so notoriously deficient in everything of that kind, that our adversaries often taunt us with it, and have held us up to public ridicule as being "without a system of philosophy based on principles inter-dependent, subordinate, and coherent." And so we were thrown on letters; thrown upon reading this and that—which anybody can do—and thus gradually getting a notion of the history of the human mind, which enables us (the "Zeit-Geist" favouring) to correct, in reading the Bible, some of the mistakes into which men of more metaphysical talents than literary experience have fallen. Cripples in like manner have been known, now and then, to be cast by their very infirmity upon some mental pursuit which has turned out happily for them; and a good fortune of this kind has perhaps been ours.

But we do not forget that this good fortune we owe to our weakness, and that the natural superiority remains with our adversaries. And some day, perhaps, the nature of God may be as well known as the nature of a cone or a triangle; and then our two bishops may deduce its properties with success, and make their brilliant logical play about it—

rightly, instead of as now, wrongly; and will resume all th
advantage. But this will hardly be in our time. So that t
superiority of this pair of distinguished metaphysicians w
never perhaps, after all, be of any real advantage to the
but they will be deluded and bemocked by it until they die